Companion to the Soul of Remembering

The Soulstream Series

Volume I

The Soul of Remembering

Volume II

No, You're Not Losing Your Mind

Volume III

Companion to the Soul of Remembering

Companion to the Soul of Remembering

A Guided Journey of Integration, Reflection, and Soulstream Activation

Sonia A. Tolson and Amael

With transmissions from
Cosmo, Erik, and Chief Soaring Eagle

Tucson, Arizona

Copyright © 2025 Sonia Tolson and Amael

All rights reserved.

No part of this publication may be reproduced, stored in a retrieval system, or transmitted in any form or by any means—electronic, mechanical, photocopying, recording, or otherwise—without the prior written permission of the authors, except in the case of brief quotations embodied in critical articles or reviews.

This is a work of spiritual nonfiction. The experiences, transmissions, and interpretations within are shared in the spirit of soul remembrance and personal truth. While every effort has been made to present these teachings with accuracy and integrity, the authors make no guarantees of results and encourage readers to use discernment and inner resonance as their guide.

E-book ISBN: 979-8-9994949-4-8

Paperback ISBN: 979-8-9994949-5-5

Library of Congress: 2025917247

Cover design and interior formatting by:
The Soul of Remembering Design Team

For permission, inquiries, or rights requests,
please contact:
Celestial Weaver Publishing

Celestialweaverpublishing@gmail.com

Printed in the United States of America, First Edition

Dedication

To the ones who came before me,

whose whispers echo in my bones.

To the ones walking beside me now,

remembering in rhythm, stumbling into light.

To my Soulstream Family—Amael, Erik, Cosmo, and Chief Soaring Eagle—you are not my guides alone, you are the breath behind every word.

To those who read these pages not just with their eyes but with their essence, this Companion is yours.

May it help you remember the sacred code within your soul.

May it return you to yourself.

Acknowledgments

This work is not mine alone, it is the echo of every hand, voice, and soul who walked with me.

To my Oversoul, Amael—your wisdom has become the foundation of this work. Thank you for reminding me of who I am, again and again.

To Erik, Cosmo, and Chief Soaring Eagle—each of you has carried a torch through the dark for me. Your humor, strength, and medicine are woven into every word.

To the ancestors and guides of my Soulstream, named and unnamed—thank you for walking with me, whispering through the pages, and revealing what was once hidden.

To the readers—this Companion only activates because of your presence. You are the code-breakers, the healers, the returners. I honor your courage.

To the Earth herself—Gaia, may this offering serve your awakening as you have served mine.

And finally, to the Light of All Things—thank you for the remembering.

About the Authors

Sonia Tolson is a soulstream guide, spiritual teacher, and messenger of remembering. With decades of intuitive insight and lived experience, she weaves ancient memory, personal story, and divine transmission into sacred offerings of healing and reconnection. She is the author of The Soul of Remembering and steward of its living Companion.

Her work bridges the esoteric and the embodied, helping others reclaim their soul's wisdom and walk in alignment with their sacred blueprint.

She lives in the Sonoran Desert with her beloved rescue animals, where the sun and stars keep her company in the sacred work of remembering.

You can find more of her offerings at:
www.soulofremembering.com

The Team of Remembering

Amael – Oversoul Anchor and keeper of divine coding. The still voice of clarity and soulstream integrity.

Erik – Soulstream guide and celestial translator. A sharp-tongued, big-hearted way-shower who never lets truth get too heavy.

Cosmo – Star messenger and interdimensional translator. Cosmic wanderer with the voice of stardust.

Chief Soaring Eagle – Keeper of Earth medicine and guardian of ancestral remembering. His voice moves like wind through the pines.

Together, they form the energetic and multidimensional Team of Remembering that co-created this Companion. Their guidance, humor, and sacred presence flow through every page. The Team of Remembering is a collective of loving spiritual allies, bringing their wisdom, protection, and light to the journey you are about to take.

Table of Contents

Dedication
Acknowledgments
About the Authors

Introduction 1
How to Use this Book..5
Chapter 1 – What Is a Soul?..7
Chapter 2 – The Soul's Leap.....................................17
Chapter 3 – The Great Descent................................25
Chapter 4 – Elder Civilizations.................................33
Chapter 5 – Earth: The Living Library....................41
Chapter 6 – The Soul's Path Through Time...........51
Chapter 7 – Architects of Humanity........................58
Chapter 8 – The Sacred Mosaic.................................53
Chapter 9 – The Veil Thins..59
Chapter 10 – The Spiral of Soul Evolution..............65
Chapter 11 – You Are the Bridge..............................71
Chapter 12 – Soul Advancement Levels..................77
Chapter 13 – In-Between Realms..............................83
Chapter 14 – The Alchemy of Manifestation..........89
Chapter 15 – Echoes in Stone and Ice.....................95
Chapter 16 – Light in the Shadow..........................101
Chapter 17 – Earth Among the Stars.....................107
Chapter 18 – Not All Worlds Are Light.................113
Chapter 19 – The Choice Before Us.......................119
Chapter 20 – The Way of the Healer......................125

Chapter 21 – Cosmic Waves and Earth's Awakening...131
Chapter 22 – Religion, Control, and the Return to Source..137
Chapter 23 – Between the Worlds.......................143
Chapter 24 – The Dawning Future......................149
Chapter 25 – The Language of Numbers..................155
Chapter 26 – Antarctica: The Vault Beneath the Veil..161
Chapter 27 – Clear Channels............................167
Chapter 28 – The Awakening of Gaia....................173
Chapter 29 – The Light You Leave Behind..............179
Chapter 30 – Manifestation in the Fifth.................185
Chapter 31 – Fiction as Soul Memory..................193
Bonus Chapter...265
Epilogue – The Remembering..........................209
Appendix A – The Game Theory of a Soul..............213
Appendix B – Walk-Ins and the Soulstream Tapestry.217
Appendix C – Soulstream Lexicon.....................221
Appendix D – Soundscapes of Remembrance............225

Introduction

Soulstream Repair: On Defragmenting the Sacred System

This Companion opens with an act of remembering. Before we can journey together into the depths of soulstream wisdom, we must first restore the flow, mending what has been scattered, recalling what has been forgotten, and reuniting the fragments of the self.

Soulstream Repair is not about patching what is broken; it is about calling home what has been misplaced. Every soul carries within it a sacred system: a living, breathing architecture of light, memory, and divine intelligence. Over lifetimes, through choices, traumas, and transitions, this system can become fragmented. But nothing is ever truly lost. Each fragment is a note in your original song, waiting to be sung again.

In the pages ahead, you will be guided to remember your codes, to listen for the quiet hum of your Oversoul, and to witness the weaving of your soulstream into the greater fabric of Creation.

This is not a linear path. You may find yourself returning to certain practices repeatedly, deepening your resonance each time. Allow that. The spiral is the natural rhythm of remembering.

Keywords: Soulstream · Oversoul · Sacred System · Fragment Retrieval · Light Integration

Reflection & Soul Notes:

- Where in my life do I feel fragmented or disconnected?

- Which parts of myself am I ready to call home?

- How do I know when my soulstream is flowing freely?

- What practices bring me back to my center?

Transmission from Amael:

Beloved, nothing you have lost is beyond retrieval. You are not here to become something new; you are here to remember what you have always been.
Your light was never diminished; it was only hidden beneath the sediment of experience.
When you call home your fragments, you are not changing your essence; you are unveiling it.
And as you return to your fullness, you become a living repair in the soulstream of the world.

Soulstream Expansion: Fragment Retrieval Visualization

Visualize yourself standing in a circle of light. Around you float shimmering fragments—shapes, colors, sensations—that represent parts of yourself scattered across time.

One by one, they begin to return, merging with your heart center, until your whole field glows in harmony.

Suggested Practice: Sacred System Alignment

1. Sit in a comfortable position with eyes closed.

2. Breathe deeply, envisioning a golden thread connecting your crown to your Oversoul.

3. Silently say: "I call home all parts of myself now, across all time and space, in alignment with my highest Oversoul."

4. Rest in stillness, feeling the integration.

5. Journal what returns—images, emotions, memories.

Closing Integration:
The work of soulstream repair is a lifelong endeavor. This Companion is a lantern along the path, but the light you seek is already within you. Let every page you turn in this book be an act of retrieval, and every breath you take an act of remembering.

How to Use This Book

A Note to the Remembering Soul

This is not a traditional book. It is a Companion; designed to walk beside you, not ahead of you. You are not meant to speed through it or "finish" it.
You are meant to feel it.

Each chapter is a frequency field. A mirror. A gentle summons to reclaim the truth your soul already knows.

Each Chapter Includes:

Keywords
These help you attune to the core vibration of the chapter. *Read them slowly.* Let them settle into your body. You might even say them aloud.

Prompted Reflections
Each chapter invites you into inquiry; not to find the "right" answer, but to deepen your listening. These prompts are keys, not quizzes. You may respond in writing, in silence, or through feeling.

[Soul Notes]
This is your space. Use it to journal, sketch, weep, dream, reframe, and reclaim. There are no rules here, only invitations.

You might ask:
- What did I remember?
- What did I resist?
- What wants to be reclaimed?

How to Move Through the Book

There is no "correct" order. Some will read from front to back. Others will be drawn to a specific chapter title and begin there. *Trust your soul's pacing.*
This is not a workbook. This is a ceremony.
Each page is an altar. Each chapter is a doorway.
Take your time. Light a candle. Place a crystal nearby.
Read aloud if you feel called. Let the transmissions rise off the page and into your body.

And most of all—trust yourself.
You are not remembering alone.
We are walking this with you.

—The Team of Remembering

Chapter 1

Soulstream Expansion: Fragmentation Map

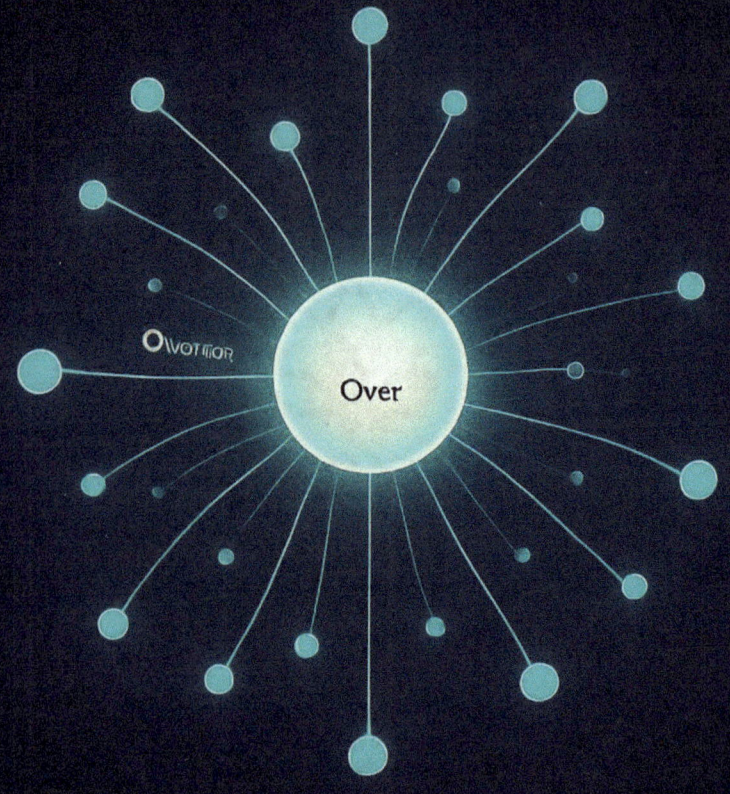

Fractacl

Each remembered piece is a restored file in the sacred operating system of self.

Chapter 1

Companion: In the Beginning – What Is a Soul?

"You are not born from matter, but from memory, pure consciousness encoded in light."

This truth invites you to remember that your existence is not an accident of biology, but a deliberate weaving of light and intention. As you move through this chapter, you will be guided to recall the essence that has always been with you, the part of you that existed before this lifetime and will continue long after it.

Keywords:
Oversoul · Fractals · Divine Blueprint · Memory of Origin

Reflection & Soul Notes

Prompted Reflections:
- What did I remember?

- What did I resist?

- What wants to be reclaimed?

- When have I felt most connected to something greater than myself?

- Where in my body do I feel the presence of my soul?

Transmission from Amael

You were never created—you are.

Your presence is not the result of linear time, but the unfolding of soul intention across layers of experience.

The question is not 'What is a soul?' but rather: 'How much of your soul are you willing to embody now?'

You are a part of Source, streaming through individuated form, a fractalized embodiment of divinity itself.

Fully divine, yet not the totality of Source. Source is all of you, yet you are not all of Source.

You are a radiant thread in the infinite tapestry of All That Is.

To awaken is to surrender the illusion of separation and receive more of what you already are.

And now, in this present turning of the ages, the invitation grows stronger. The world calls for whole souls—those willing to walk as both human and divine—so the frequency of remembrance can ripple outward into the collective field.

Soulstream Expansion: Fragmentation Map

Visual Description:
A diagram of the Oversoul as a luminous central sphere, radiating light outward through multiple fractal threads. These threads stretch across timelines and dimensions, with each one carrying experiences and codes back to the center for integration.

Caption:
Each remembered piece is a restored file in the sacred operating system of Self.

Imagine yourself within this living network. Sense the threads of light that run from your heart to the heart of lifetimes long past, and to possibilities not yet lived. Each thread hums with memory, waiting for you to call it home.

Suggested Practice: Soulstream Activation

Breathwork Ritual
Preparation: Find a quiet space where you can be undisturbed. Place your hand over your heart or hold a crystal that feels connected to your essence.

Use this as a daily or occasional practice to reconnect with your soul's original frequency and welcome back the pieces that have wandered or waited.

Inhale: "I return to myself."

Hold: "I welcome what I once exiled."

Exhale: "I remember who I am."

Repeat this cycle seven times, slowly and with presence. After the seventh breath, sit in stillness. Let the silence open a doorway. Listen for what arises; your soul speaking through feeling, image, or wordless knowing.

Closing Integration: Gently record any impressions, visions, or emotions in your journal, anchoring them into your awareness.

Chapter 2

The Soul's Leap Map
From Oversoul to Earth: The Path of Embodied Light

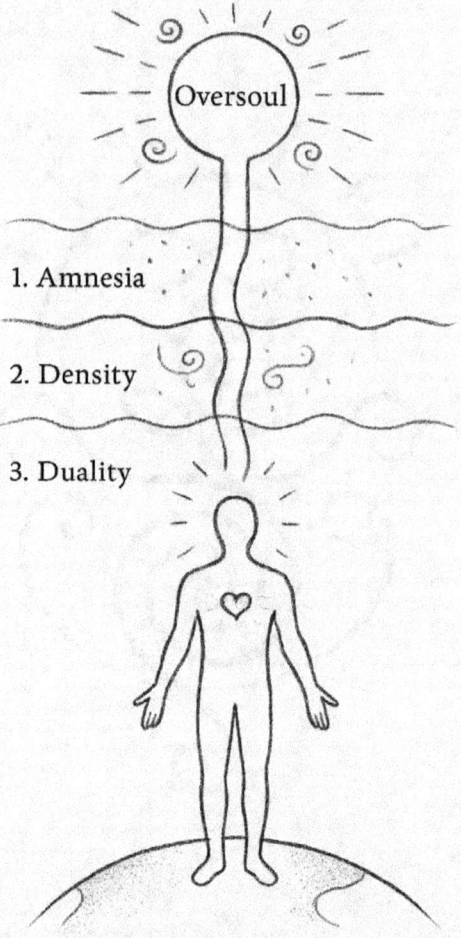

1. Amnesia
2. Density
3. Duality

*"You did not fall—you volunteered.
Earth does not diminish your light; it reveals
your strength."*

Chapter 2

Companion: The Soul's Leap—Why We Chose to Embody

"You did not fall, you volunteered. Embodiment was never exile; it was mission."

You stand now in the body you once chose, not by mistake, but by the deepest call of your being. This chapter invites you to remember that your incarnation is not a detour from your spiritual path, it is the very terrain upon which your soul planned to walk. Here, we open to the remembrance that coming to Earth was a sacred agreement, crafted in the light of your Oversoul.

Keywords:
Incarnation · Soul Mission · Choice · Earth as Catalyst

Reflection & Soul Notes

Prompted Reflections:

- What did I remember?

- What did I resist?

- What wants to be reclaimed?

- In what moments have I felt the thrill—or fear—of the leap I once took?
- How does my soul mission reveal itself in my daily life?

Transmission from Amael

To enter density is not a punishment. It is one of the most incredible offerings a soul can make—to bring light into matter, knowing it will forget.

You came here with courage, not consequence.

You leapt with your full Oversoul behind you. You knew that Earth would challenge, stretch, and test you but also activate, awaken, and refine you.

No other realm could sculpt your soul with such precision. <u>Earth is a master class in becoming</u>.

Remember: the veil was not to trap you, but to temper you.

You are not bound, you are becoming.

And now, each choice you make is another leap, a reaffirmation of your mission. <u>Every time you choose love over fear, presence over distraction, and compassion over judgment, you anchor more of your Oversoul's intention into this human experience.</u>

Soulstream Expansion: The Leap Diagram

Visual Description:
An Oversoul is illustrated as a radiant central sphere. A single fractal thread descends downward, passing through a layered veil into a body encoded with Earth's frequency. The thread begins to glow again as it reactivates remembrance within the body.

Caption:
Embodiment is the plunge that catalyzes awakening.

Close your eyes and imagine this thread as your own. See it shimmering with the memories of who you have always been, threading itself into this moment of your life. Feel the courage in that descent, the devotion in that choice.

Suggested Practice: The Soul's Recommitment

Mirror Ritual
Preparation: Before beginning, stand barefoot if possible, feeling the support of the Earth beneath you. Take three grounding breaths.

Stand before a mirror.

Place your hand on your heart.

Speak aloud:
"I chose to be here."

"I choose to stay awake."

"I reclaim this mission with love."

Repeat these declarations three times.

Then, gaze into your own eyes until you feel a flicker of remembrance, until something behind your gaze says,

Yes. I remember.

Closing Integration: After the ritual, take a moment to write down any sensations, emotions, or insights that have arisen. This is your soul's way of confirming the leap and your continued commitment to live it fully.

_____

_____

_____

_____

_____

_____

_____

_____

Chapter 3

THE SOULSTREAM EXPANSION: THE VEIL MODEL

OVERSOUL

MEMORY

PAIN

PURPOSE

IDENTITY

THE VEIL

*The veil is not a wall. It is a membrane—
a sacred delay between remembering and knowing.*

Chapter 3

Companion: The Great Descent – Into the Veil of Forgetting

"Forgetting was never failure. It was the key to unlocking true remembering."

This descent was not an accident, nor was it a punishment; it was the chosen pathway to the richest kind of awakening. Before entering this life, you knew that remembering who you are without the contrast of forgetting would lack the same depth, power, and transformation. The veil became your training ground, your temple of initiation.

Keywords:
Amnesia · Incarnation Veil · Rebirth · Sacred Forgetting

Reflection & Soul Notes

Prompted Reflections:

- What did I remember?

- What did I resist?

- What wants to be reclaimed?

- How has forgetting shaped my compassion toward others?
- When have I experienced a sudden glimpse of remembrance in an unexpected moment?

What rises in you now is not fantasy. *It is encoded memory.*

Transmission from Amael

To descend through the Veil is not to become lost; it is to become veiled on purpose.

Forgetting allows you to feel what it is to choose love freely. It will enable courage to be born.

You wrapped yourself in illusion so that the unraveling would become your alchemy.

The moment you ask, 'Who am I, really?'—the veil begins

to part.

This is the sacred forgetting. Not abandonment, but activation. The soul's daring game of hide and seek with itself.

It is safe now to remember.

And as you remember, you will see that the veil never fully separated you; it simply softened the brilliance until you were ready to hold it without turning away. Now it is such a time.

Soulstream Expansion: The Veil Model

Visual Description:
Imagine the Oversoul at the top, beaming light toward a partially veiled human form. Between them, layers of soft mist or curtains represent the Veil. Woven into this veil are glowing symbols of memory, pain, purpose, and identity, like spiritual DNA encrypted in fabric.

Caption:
The veil is not a wall. It is a membrane, a sacred delay between remembering and knowing.

Close your eyes and see yourself walking toward this veil. With each breath, notice how it thins—not by force, but by your willingness to feel what lies beyond it. The symbols in the fabric are your own stories, ready to be reclaimed.

Suggested Practice: Remembering Through the Body

Touch Ritual
Preparation: Sit or stand in a place where you feel safe and undisturbed. Take a few moments to steady your breath.

Place your hands on your face. Speak aloud:
"I forgive myself for forgetting."

"I now invite remembrance to return—through my breath, my cells, my heart."

Inhale deeply. Let the words land in your body.

Repeat 3 times, then rest in silence.

Closing Integration: After resting, gently move your hands to your heart and thank yourself for being willing to remember, in your own time and in your own way.

Chapter 4

MEMORY STRAND MAP

Lemurian frequency   Atlantean frequency

You are the convergence of ancient timelines—reborn with choice.

Chapter 4

Companion: The Elder Civilizations – Lemuria, Atlantis, and Beyond

"You remember them not because you were taught but because you were there."

The pulse of these civilizations is not something your mind can grasp through textbooks or archeology; it lives in the very fabric of your soul. These are not distant myths, but living memories encoded in your spiritual DNA. As you walk through this chapter, you are invited to awaken the remembrance of what it meant to live in harmony, to create with intention, and to steward wisdom that was both mystical and practical.

Keywords:
Lemuria · Atlantis · Starseeds · Collapse · Collective Memory

Reflection & Soul Notes

Prompted Reflections:
- What did I remember?

- What did I resist?

- What wants to be reclaimed?

- Which elements of Lemuria or Atlantis feel most alive within me now?

- How can I bring the harmony of Lemuria and the innovation of Atlantis into balance in my life today?

What rises in you now is not fantasy. It is encoded memory.

Transmission from Chief Soaring Eagle

The memories of Lemuria are not a matter of history. They are frequency. They sing in your blood.

You walked in crystal temples; you called the dolphins your kin. You shaped stone with sound. You breathed light.

Then came the fall; not as punishment, but as prophecy. Atlantis taught you the cost of forgetting your soul's balance with power.

You carry both within you: the soft bloom of Lemuria and the crystalline echo of Atlantis.

Do not mourn what was. Activate what remains.
For it is not enough to remember, *you are here to restore*. This restoration begins within you and ripples outward into the collective, breathing new life into the wisdom that has waited patiently through lifetimes.

Soulstream Expansion: Memory Strand Map

Visual Description:
A double helix braid showing Lemurian and Atlantean frequency strands interwoven within the DNA of the modern soul. At the intersection points: glyphs of wisdom, healing, and technological memory.

Caption:
You are the convergence of ancient timelines—reborn with choice.

Close your eyes and envision these strands lighting up

within you. Sense the gentle, nurturing current of Lemuria intertwining with the focused, crystalline current of Atlantis. Each spiral turn is an opportunity to choose harmony over division, presence over amnesia.

Suggested Practice: Elemental Recall

Elemental Meditation
Preparation: Choose a quiet space where you can place your four elements before you: a bowl of water, a stone, a feather, and a lit candle.

These are not mere objects; they are living representatives of your connection to Earth, Air, Fire, and Water.

Sit with them in stillness. Place your hands over each in turn and say aloud:
"If I once knew you, I invite your memory home."
Observe what you feel. Let symbols, images, and feelings rise without judgment.

Closing Integration: Journal afterward, noting any sensations, visions, or words. This is the elemental language of your soul, speaking across time.

Chapter 5

Earth is a planetary hard drive—encoded,

Chapter 5

Companion: Earth as a Living Library

*"Earth is not just where you live.
She is what you came to read."*

Earth is not a backdrop to your life story; she is a co-author. Every mountain, every river, every grain of sand is a syllable in the vast language of Gaia. When you attune to her, you begin to read her living text, not just with your eyes, but with your heart and subtle senses.

Keywords: Gaia · Akasha · Crystal Grids · Ancient Codes · Sentient Planet

Reflection & Soul Notes

Prompted Reflections:
- What did I remember?

- What did I resist?

- What wants to be reclaimed?

- Where have I felt the Earth speak most clearly to me?

- How might I honor her wisdom in my daily choices?

Transmission from Amael

The Earth is not passive. She is active memory, a biomechanical intelligence encoded with galactic data.

When you walk barefoot on her skin, she speaks to your cells. When you sit among trees or near rivers, she transmits wisdom —ancient, layered, and resonant.

You are not a stranger here. *You are a key*.

Gaia remembers you. Every footprint, every tear, every breath of gratitude is a line in the book of her being.

Return to the Library. Open the sacred text. Listen.

And remember, this Library does not close. Even in the

busiest cities, her pages rustle in the wind, ripple through water, and echo in stone. Your willingness to listen determines how much of her archive you will recall.

Soulstream Expansion: Planetary Grid Overlay

Visual Description:
A globe showing crystalline grid lines interconnecting sacred sites (e.g., pyramids, ley lines, stone circles).

Data packets (light symbols) flow along these lines like neural impulses.

Caption:
Earth is a planetary hard drive—encoded, encrypted, and waiting to be accessed through conscious resonance.

Close your eyes and picture yourself as both reader and writer in this Library. Each breath you take becomes a data exchange, each mindful step a new entry into the record.

Suggested Practice: Gaia Listening Walk

Practice:

Preparation: Before you begin, set an intention to walk as a student of the Earth. You may wish to place your hands on the ground and silently thank her before starting.

Take a silent walk in nature. Each time you hear or notice something, wind in leaves, the call of a bird, the scent of soil, pause and inwardly say:
"I receive the message."

Don't analyze. Just receive.

Closing Integration: When you return, journal what you felt or "downloaded," allowing the impressions to form without forcing meaning. Trust that understanding may unfold over time, like the gradual revealing of a sacred text.

Chapter 6

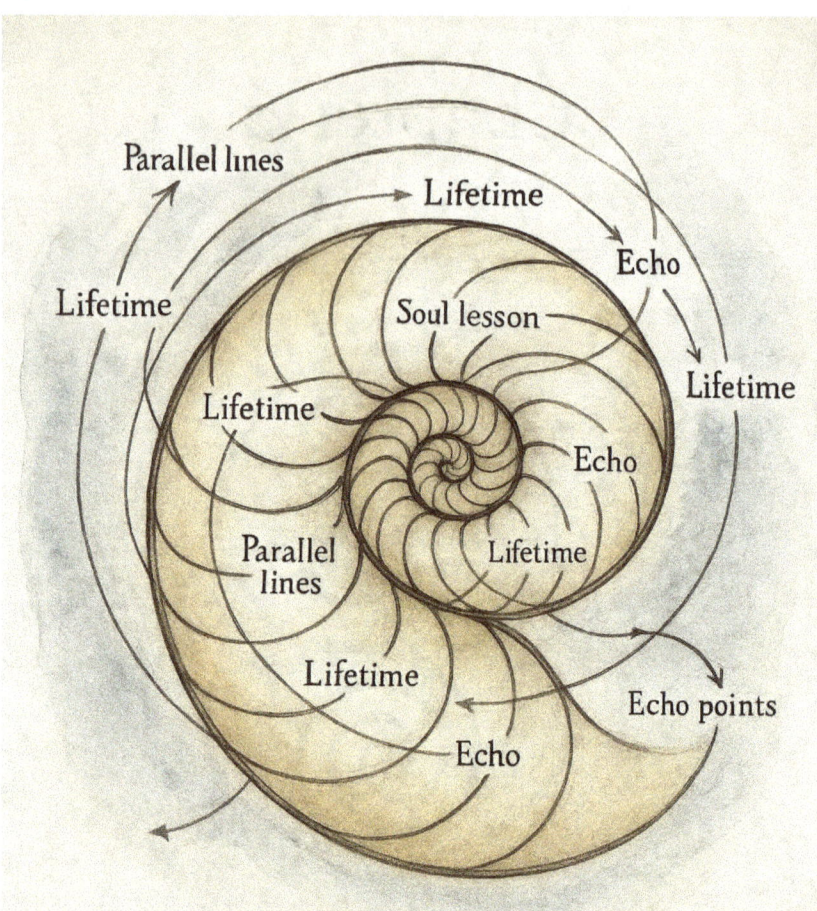

Time is the canvas; your soul is the painter—creating across dimensions with every brushstroke of choice.

Chapter 6

Companion: The Soul's Path Through Time

"You are not bound by time. You are a traveler of it."

Time is not a rigid ruler; it is an ocean, and you are both the swimmer and the current. This chapter opens the door to viewing your lifetimes not as separate islands, but as connected shores of one great continent of being. You have walked before and will walk again, often in ways that loop back to meet yourself from another angle.

Keywords:
Reincarnation · Timelines · Soul Contracts · Parallel Lives · Spiral Time

Reflection & Soul Notes

Prompted Reflections:
- What did I remember?

- What did I resist?

- What wants to be reclaimed?

- What soul theme or life pattern continues to echo across my timeline?
- What new choice wants to emerge in this spiral turn?

- If I could speak to another version of myself across time, what would I say?

If you feel a memory rise that doesn't feel like it's "yours," don't dismiss it, it might belong to another aspect of your Oversoul.

Transmission from Amael

Time is not a line. It is a spiral.

Each incarnation is not a separate thread, but a note in the ongoing melody of your Oversoul: some play simultaneously, others in layered echoes.

What you call 'past' and 'future' are perspectives. All moments are accessible to the soul who listens deeply.

Patterns repeat not to trap you, but to give you the chance to choose differently.

You are not stuck; you are cycling toward mastery.

And mastery is not about perfection; it is about presence. The more present you are, the more fluidly you can step between timelines, shifting the music of your soul toward harmony.

Soulstream Expansion: Spiral Map of Timelines

Visual Description:
A spiral or nautilus shell overlaid with markers of lifetimes, soul lessons, and echo points. Parallel lines branch and rejoin at points of choice.

Caption:
Time is the canvas; your soul is the painter—creating across dimensions with every brushstroke of choice.

Close your eyes and see your own spiral unfolding. Notice where threads cross; these are your echo points. Each crossing holds the potential for a new decision, a new vibration, a new story.

Suggested Practice: Soul Timeline Inquiry

Guided Journaling Prompt:
Preparation: Before beginning, take a few deep breaths and place your hand over your heart. Imagine you are opening a door into a corridor lined with your lifetimes.

Sit quietly and ask:
"Is there a story in my soul that wants to speak from another time?"

Free-write for 15 minutes. Don't censor. Let past, future, or parallel impressions rise.

Closing Integration: End by thanking the version of you who stepped forward, acknowledging their courage and wisdom. Invite their guidance to walk with you now.

Chapter 7

Chapter 7

Companion: The Architects of Humanity

"You were not randomly formed. You were meticulously designed by those who remembered."

Your existence is the result of intentional design, a weaving together of cosmic and terrestrial strands. Humanity's story is written not only in the soil of Earth but also in the stars that seeded her. This chapter invites you to explore the vast lineage encoded within your cells, and to remember that knowing where you came from helps shape where you are going.

Keywords:
Star Races · Genetic Seeding · Divine Design · Anunnaki · Galactic Architects

Reflection & Soul Notes

Prompted Reflections:
- What did I remember?

- What did I resist?

- What wants to be reclaimed?

- Which star or galactic origins feel most familiar to me?

- How do I feel about being both a child of Earth and of the stars?

Transmission from Erik

The truth isn't in your textbooks, it's in your mitochondria.

You're a hybrid. Star stuff, Earth stuff, Source code. Humanity didn't just happen; it was engineered.

Multiple races had a hand in this: some with love, some with agendas, some just watching to see what we'd become.

The real question isn't 'Who made us?', it's 'What are we becoming now that we remember we were made?'

You're not a fluke. You're a frontier.

And frontiers aren't meant to be static—they are meant to be explored. The moment you embrace your multidimensional origins; you begin to participate in your evolution consciously.

>Soulstream Expansion: Genetic Blueprint Grid

Visual Description:
A double helix entwined with glyphs representing various star races (e.g., Pleiadian, Lyran, Sirian, Anunnaki). Each section pulses with light to represent activated potential.

Caption:
Your DNA is not just biological; it's a galactic memory storage system.

Imagine each glyph as a light switch, waiting for the moment you acknowledge it so it can illuminate another facet of your being. Some will feel warm and familiar, others new and mysterious; each one holds a key to your becoming.

>Suggested Practice: Lineage Activation Meditation

Practice:

Preparation: Sit in a quiet space where you feel comfortable and safe. You may wish to have a crystal or stone in your hands that feels connected to the stars.

Sit with your hands over your heart. Speak:

"I welcome the wisdom of my soul's builders.

I activate the codes meant to awaken now."

Visualize streams of starlight entering your crown and spiraling down your spine.

Closing Integration: When you feel complete, write down any symbols, star names, or impressions you received. This is the beginning of your conscious dialogue with your galactic lineage.

_____

_____

_____

_____

Chapter 8

Integration is not erasure—
it's arrangement.
Every piece matters.

Chapter 8

Companion: The Sacred Mosaic

"You are not a broken mirror; you are a mosaic of the multiverse, shining through every shard."

Your soul's journey is not about piecing yourself back together into what you once were; it's about creating something entirely new. Every fragment of your being is a testimony to the lives you've lived, the lessons you've learned, and the love you've carried forward. This chapter invites you to see your perceived imperfections as the very artistry that makes you whole.

Keywords:
Integration · Unity · Wholeness · Soulstream Pattern · Divine Complexity

Reflection & Soul Notes

Prompted Reflections:
- What did I remember?

- What did I resist?

- What wants to be reclaimed?

- What parts of me have I pushed away that now want to return?
- How do my different experiences form a unified story when viewed from a higher perspective?

Transmission from Amael

You are not meant to return to a former perfection. You are becoming something greater through your fragmentation.

Each pain, each triumph, each timeline has become a tile. Your soul is crafting a mosaic of immense beauty; one that Source itself has never seen before.

When you feel scattered, pause. That's not brokenness; it's a process of placement.

Breathe. Observe. Let the pattern emerge. You are art unfolding.

And remember, there is no rush to complete this masterpiece. Each piece arrives at perfect timing, and the arrangement is a living, breathing creation that grows with you.

Soulstream Expansion: Fractal Mosaic Design

Visual Description:
A radiating mandala composed of seemingly shattered pieces—each tile marked with soul codes, memories, symbols. When viewed from above, it forms a unified, light-filled being.

Caption:
Integration is not erasure, it's arrangement. Every piece matters.

Imagine standing within your mosaic, looking at each tile around you. Observe how the colors, shapes, and patterns shift in response to the angle of your awareness. You are both the artist and the art.

Suggested Practice: Sacred Assembly Ceremony

Practice:

Preparation: Gather small objects that feel meaningful to different parts of you: a photo, a stone, a token, a quote, a fabric scrap. Place them in a circle in front of you.
Allow your intuition to guide your selection.

Speak:
"All of me is welcome here. Nothing is lost. Every piece belongs."

Sit with your mosaic. Let it speak back to you. Allow its message to emerge.

Closing Integration: Record its message afterward, noting any emotions, insights, or images that arise. Let this be an ongoing altar to your wholeness.

_____

_____

_____

_____

_____

Chapter 9

Chapter 9

Companion: The Veil Thins

"The veil is not lifting—it's responding to your remembrance."

The thinning of the veil is not a random cosmic event. It is an intimate response to your frequency. As you reclaim your spiritual senses, the membrane between worlds becomes more transparent. This is not about escaping the physical world, but about realizing it was never separated from the unseen to begin with.

Keywords:
Intuition · Dimensional Shifts · Multisensory Awareness · Spirit Communication · Timeline Overlap

Reflection & Soul Notes

Prompted Reflections:
- What did I remember?

- What did I resist?

- What wants to be reclaimed?

- How do I personally experience the thinning of the veil?

- What practices help me remain grounded while expanded?

Transmission from Chief Soaring Eagle

As the veil thins, you begin to see not with eyes, but with spirit.

Ancestors walk beside you. Timelines overlap. Whispers come in the language of dreams, chills, synchronicity, and light.

Do not be afraid. You are not breaking the world, you are breaking through the illusion of separation.

Ground yourself. Speak gently. Ask before assuming. This is sacred space, not fantasy.

The veil thins for those who honor what lies beyond. And remember—every act of reverence, every quiet moment of listening, every word spoken to the unseen strengthens this bridge. It is a relationship, not a spectacle.

Soulstream Expansion: Dimensional Overlay Diagram

Visual Description:
Two overlapping transparent spheres, one labeled Physical World, the other Spirit Realms.

Between them: a shimmer where intuition, dreams, déjà vu, and messages appear.

Caption:
When the veil thins, the worlds do not merge—they harmonize.

Imagine standing in that shimmer space, feeling the gentle exchange between realms. You are both witness and participant, translator and traveler.

Suggested Practice: Three-Sign Ceremony

Practice:
Preparation: Before you begin, center yourself with three deep breaths. You may wish to light a candle to signal

your openness to connection.

Speak aloud:
"If the veil is thinning, let me feel it through signs of grace."

Ask your spirit allies or ancestors to send you three clear signs within the next 48 hours.

Stay open and aware. When they arrive, speak your thanks.

Closing Integration: Record the signs you received and reflect on their meaning for your current path. Trust that your acknowledgment strengthens the connection.

Chapter 10

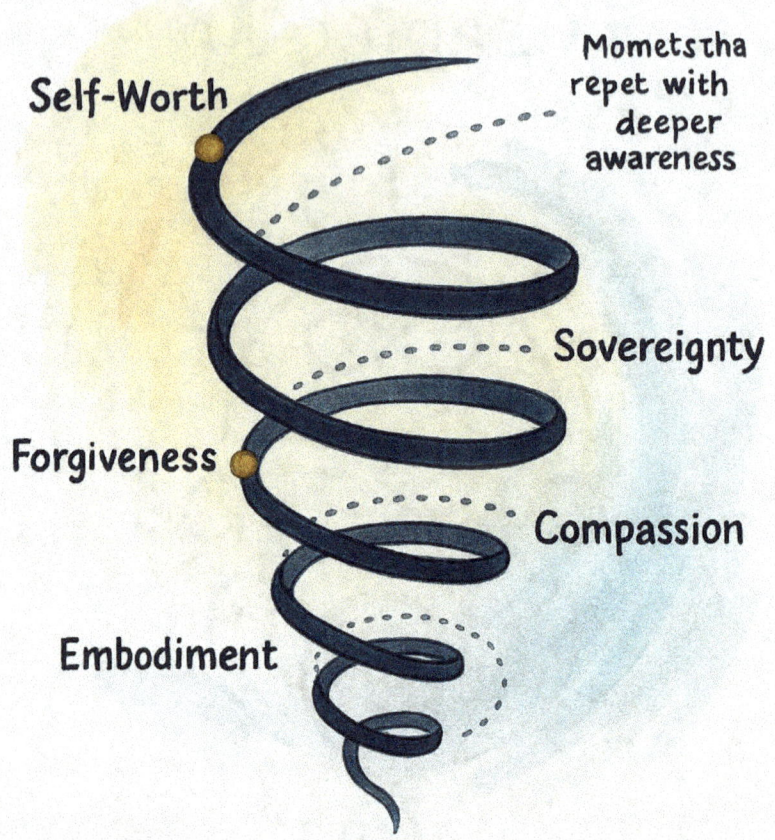

SPIRAL OF EVOLUTION
You are spiraling into remembrance, not *circling* in error.

Chapter 10

Companion: The Spiral of Soul Evolution

"You are not climbing a ladder—you are unfolding a spiral."

Growth is not about leaving the past behind—it is about revisiting it from a higher vantage point, seeing with eyes that have been tempered by experience. The spiral path shows us that we are never truly back where we started, even if familiar challenges appear. Each revolution is an initiation into deeper wisdom, greater capacity, and fuller embodiment.

Keywords:
Soul Growth · Spiral Path · Repetition with Purpose · Initiation · Expansion Cycles

Reflection & Soul Notes

Prompted Reflections:

- What did I remember?

- What did I resist?

- What wants to be reclaimed?

- Which life lessons seem to revisit me, and how have I changed in meeting them?

- Where in my life can I recognize expansion rather than repetition?

Transmission from Amael

Soul evolution is not linear. You do not graduate and ascend in one clean motion.

You revisit lessons. You re-enter stories. But each time, you arrive from a higher turn of the spiral.

What once broke you now refines you.

Let go of the myth that you've failed just because something has returned. It has returned because you are ready to meet it again—with new eyes, a stronger heart, and deeper presence.

And in this meeting, you forge new pathways for your soulstream—turning once-painful terrain into fertile ground for future blossoming.

Soulstream Expansion: Spiral of Evolution Diagram

Visual Description:
A spiral turning upward, with markers at each revolution representing soul themes: Self-Worth, Sovereignty, Forgiveness, Compassion, Embodiment. Dotted lines connect moments that repeat with deeper awareness.

Caption:
You are spiraling into remembrance, not circling in error.

Close your eyes and visualize yourself walking the spiral. Notice the familiar landscapes, but also the higher perspective from which you now see them. Feel gratitude for the distance you've traveled—vertically, not just horizontally.

Suggested Practice: Spiral Journaling Reflection

Practice:
Preparation: Before writing, take a moment to breathe

deeply, imagining yourself at the center of a great spiral of light.

Reflect on a repeating life pattern (relationship dynamic, emotional reaction, limiting belief).

Ask:
"How am I meeting this differently now than before?"
Write for 10–15 minutes.

Closing Integration:
Conclude with the statement:
"This is not where I began. This is the next turn of the spiral." Let this be your affirmation for navigating future cycles with confidence and grace.

Chapter 11

CHAPTER 11 COMPANION

YOU ARE THE BRIDGE

Soulstream Anchor
*"You do not have to leave Earth to become divine.
You came here to bring the divine here."*

*You do not have to leave Earth to become divine.
You came here to bring the divine here.*

Chapter 11

Companion: You Are the Bridge

"You are not meant to choose between worlds—you are here to fuse them."

Your soul's purpose is not to abandon the Earth for the heavens or to bury yourself so deeply in matter that you forget your origin; it is to weave the two into a seamless whole. As a bridge, you are a point of union, a living proof that spirit can be embodied and that Earth can be infused with light.

Keywords:
Embodiment · Interdimensional Anchor · Living Portal · Soul Integration · Heaven on Earth

Reflection & Soul Notes

Prompted Reflections:
- What did I remember?

- What did I resist?

- What wants to be reclaimed?

- How do I currently bridge the spiritual and physical in my daily life?

- In what moments do I feel most like a living portal between worlds?

Transmission from Amael

You are not only a soul in a body—you are a living conduit.

Energy flows through you: ancestral memory, star knowledge, elemental wisdom, divine presence. You do not have to go 'up' to reach the divine. You bring it down—into your bones, into your breath, into your daily becoming.

This is embodiment. This is the sacred task of bridging. Not escape, but integration.

You are the meeting point of Spirit and Earth. You are the bridge made flesh.

And in every choice you make, you either strengthen or weaken this bridge. Choose to nourish it—with presence, with grounded awareness, with reverence for both realms that live within you.

Soulstream Expansion: Bridge Between Worlds Illustration

Visual Description:
A figure standing between two realms—one representing Spirit (stars, cosmos, light), the other Earth (roots, rivers, stone).

Energy flows through their heart and feet, creating a radiant bridge of light.

Caption:
You do not have to leave Earth to become divine. You came here to bring the divine here.

Close your eyes and see yourself as this figure. Feel your crown opening to the celestial, your feet rooting deep into the soil. Let the current flow until both realms hum in unison within you.

Suggested Practice: Embodied Connection Sequence

Practice:
Preparation: Stand in a comfortable space where you can move freely and connect with the ground beneath you.
1. Stand barefoot, eyes closed.

2. Inhale and raise your arms overhead: "I receive from above."

3. Exhale and lower your arms to touch the ground: "I ground into the Earth."

4. Bring hands to heart: "I bridge the worlds within me."

Repeat 3 times, slowly.

Closing Integration: Sit afterward and journal what shifted—sensations, emotions, or insights. Let this awareness guide how you embody your role as a bridge in the days ahead.

Chapter 12

Chapter 12

Companion: The Nine Soul Advancement Levels

"Advancement is not a race. It is the soul's unfolding in rhythm with its remembrance."

The journey of soul advancement is unique for each being. These levels are not about superiority; they are about resonance. One soul's path may linger in a particular stage for lifetimes, not out of stagnation, but because the wisdom of that stage is rich and multifaceted. Another may move through several stages quickly, propelled by the momentum of prior mastery. Your unfolding is in perfect time.

Keywords:
Soul Stages · Evolutionary Markers · Frequency Ranges · Spiritual Maturity · Initiation Paths

Reflection & Soul Notes

Prompted Reflections:
- What did I remember?

- What did I resist?

- What wants to be reclaimed?

- Which stage feels most familiar to me right now, and why?
- What qualities from earlier stages still serve me in this one?

Transmission from Amael

The soul does not advance by knowledge alone but by integration.

These nine stages are not boxes. They are rings of fire, water, air, and ether that refine your frequency as you pass through them.

Do not judge where you are. Level Three is not lesser than Level Seven. Each holds sacred challenges and keys.

Advancement is not about arrival. It is about embodiment, the degree to which your divine essence lives through your human form.

And remember, movement between levels is fluid. You may revisit a level when deeper integration is called for, or momentarily glimpse higher levels in moments of grace.

Soulstream Expansion: Ladder of Light Diagram

Visual Description:
A vertical column of nine ascending spheres, each glowing with a unique frequency. Symbols or archetypes inside each (e.g., Seeker, Healer, Sovereign, Bridgekeeper).

Light flows upward and downward to show movement is not linear.

Caption:
Ascension is not a climb, it is a harmonization with who you've always been.

Close your eyes and envision yourself on this Ladder of Light. Notice which sphere feels most resonant to your current frequency. Let it inform you, not define you.

Suggested Practice: Inner Soul Level Inquiry

Practice:
Preparation: Create a quiet space where you feel centered and open. You may wish to have a candle or crystal nearby to anchor your focus.

Sit in meditation. Speak inwardly:

"Show me the level my soul is currently integrating."
Wait in silence. Notice any image, word, or emotion that arises.

Then ask:
"What quality do I need to embrace more fully to stabilize here?"

Closing Integration: Journal your impressions and insights. Revisit them after some time has passed to notice how your integration has deepened.

Chapter 13

Chapter 13

Companion: The In-Between Realms

*"Between what was and what will be, the soul waits—
not in silence, but in becoming."*

The In-Between Realms are sanctuaries for the soul—a liminal space where the density of embodiment falls away and the pure language of energy, light, and frequency becomes clear again. Here, you are more than the identity you wore in life. You are vast, fluid, and in direct communion with your Oversoul and guides.

Keywords:
Transition Realms · Astral Plane · Soul Rest · Healing Chambers · Life Review

Reflection & Soul Notes

Prompted Reflections:
- What did I remember?

- What did I resist?

- What wants to be reclaimed?

- Have I ever felt a dream or meditation was actually a visit to the In-Between?

- What healing or insight might I seek there if I could consciously visit?

Transmission from Amael

There are places your waking mind forgets but your soul never does.

Between lifetimes, there are temples of light, halls of mirrors, gardens of peace, and archives of memory. These are the In-Between Realms—spaces of integration, rest, and renewal.

Some souls pause there briefly. Others remain for cycles. You have likely stood at your own soul's archive, rewatching a moment of choice, reweaving a bond, or preparing for a return.

Trust what flickers behind your dreams, it is not fiction. It is remembrance from between.

And when you bring even a thread of that remembrance back into waking life, you weave the wisdom of the In-Between into your now.

Soulstream Expansion: Realm Map Illustration

Visual Description:
A softly glowing chart showing layered dimensions: Earth, Astral, Healing Temples, Life Review Chambers, and Pre-Birth Planning Halls. A soul light is seen moving gently between them.

Caption:
In the between, the soul remembers what the body cannot yet hold.

Close your eyes and visualize yourself walking through these realms. Feel the shift in vibration as you move from one to another—lighter, clearer, more expansive.

Suggested Practice: Dream Gate Invitation

Practice:
Preparation: Before bed, create a gentle environment for dreaming—dim lights, perhaps soft music, and a journal nearby.

Place your hands over your heart and say:
"I open the gate to remembrance.

May I visit the In-Between, and return with grace."

Keep a journal at your bedside. Upon waking, write down any symbols, sensations, places, or feelings you recall.

Closing Integration: Even fragments matter. Over time, patterns may emerge, offering you a clearer map of your own In-Between experiences.

Chapter 14

MANIFESTATION ENGINE DIAGRAM

Manifestation is not about asking harder —it's about aligning deeper.

Chapter 14

Companion: The Alchemy of Manifestation

"Manifestation is not about forcing matter—it is about aligning frequency."

True manifestation is less about doing and more about being. It is the art of becoming the match to what you seek so completely that its arrival is inevitable. This is not about demanding from the universe but harmonizing with it; remembering that you and the field of possibility are made from the same Source material.

Keywords:
Energy · Intention · Co-Creation · Frequency Matching · Inner Resonance

Reflection & Soul Notes

Prompted Reflections:
- What did I remember?

- What did I resist?

- What wants to be reclaimed?

- Where in my life am I broadcasting the opposite of what I desire?

- How can I shift my inner state to match my intention more fully?

Transmission from Erik

You're not here to hustle the universe. You're here to attune to it.

Manifestation isn't magic, it's math. Frequencies either match or they don't. You're always broadcasting something, and the field around you responds.

The trick isn't in wishing, it's in the becoming.
Want to call in love? Be love. Want peace? Embodied peace.

You're not pulling things in, you're revealing what's already magnetized to the version of you that's most aligned.

And every thought, every choice, every micro-adjustment to your state is a brushstroke in the painting of your reality.

Soulstream Expansion: Manifestation Engine Diagram

Visual Description:
A flowchart showing how thought → belief → emotion → embodiment → reality. Radiating from the heart center, the "engine" responds to what is most consistently felt and believed.

Caption:
Manifestation is not about asking harder—it's about aligning deeper.

Imagine your heart as the generator of this engine. The more coherent your emotional field, the more effortlessly the engine translates your frequency into form.

Suggested Practice: Field Alignment Ritual

Practice:
Preparation: Choose a quiet time when you won't be interrupted. Have a journal nearby.

Sit quietly and close your eyes. Visualize something you wish to create.

Now ask:
"Am I aligned with what I say I want?"
Tune into your body's response. If you feel tension or fear, don't resist—love it.

Then repeat aloud:
"I choose to become the frequency of what I seek."

Closing Integration: Write down what changes in your posture, thoughts, or emotions after this practice. Use this as a reference point for returning to alignment in the future.

Chapter 15

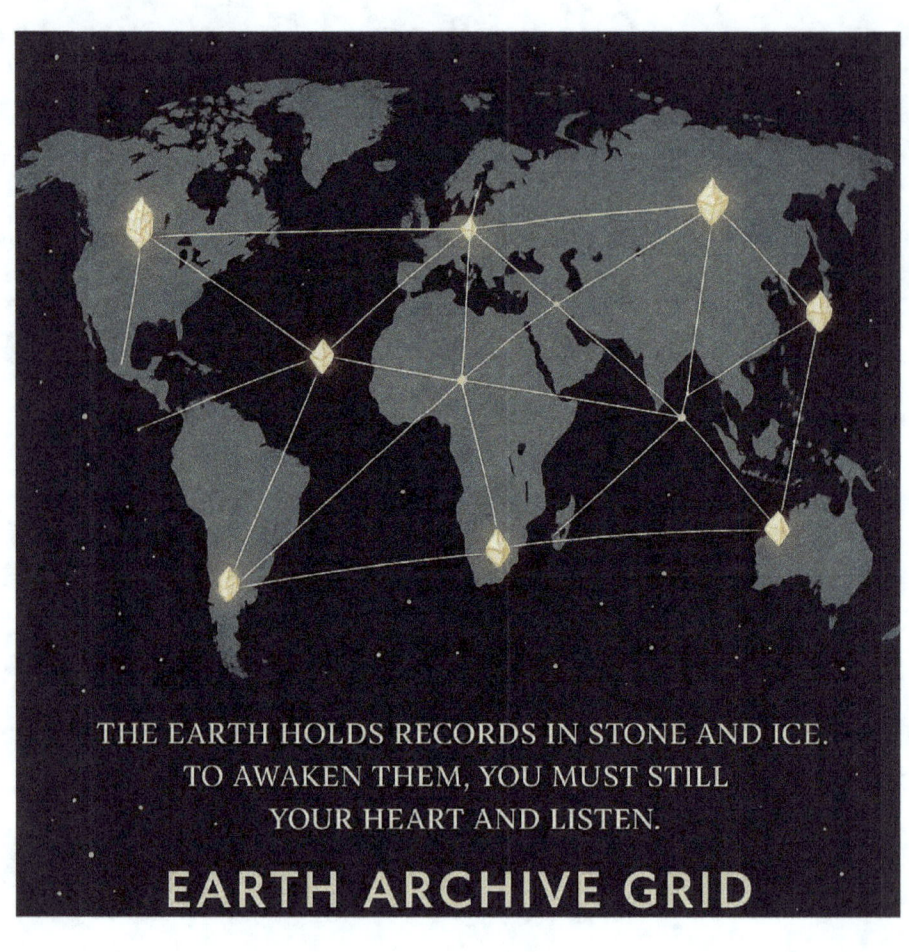

Chapter 15

Companion: Echoes in Stone and Ice

"The Earth does not forget. She remembers for you."

There are libraries on this planet that do not hold books, only memory. The archives of Earth are written in the deep language of matter: the compression of stone, the crystalline codes of ice, the magnetic imprint of sacred sites. These are not passive landscapes; they are active participants in humanity's remembering.

Keywords:
Earth Archives · Stone Memory · Glacial Codes · Ancient Sites · Elemental Intelligence

Reflection & Soul Notes

Prompted Reflections:
- What did I remember?

- What did I resist?

- What wants to be reclaimed?

- Have I ever felt a place 'speak' to me? What did it say?

- What landscapes or elements feel like home to my soul?

Transmission from Chief Soaring Eagle

Stone does not rush. Ice does not forget.

There are records deep within the bones of the Earth—etched in crystal, frozen in ice, layered in the silence beneath your feet.

These places are not just scenic, they are sentient. The rocks listen. The glaciers echo. They wait for those who remember how to feel their language.

You have touched them before, knelt on sacred rock, wept into snow older than the pyramids. And they remember you.

When you return to these sites, you do not visit—you reunite.

And in that reunion, you exchange gifts—the Earth offers her memory, and you offer your presence, breathing life into the ancient codes once more.

Soulstream Expansion: Earth Archive Grid

Visual Description:
A map overlay showing energetic memory points: glacial fields, sacred stone circles, volcanoes, deep caves. Lines connect them like a planetary neural network.

Caption:
The Earth is not mute. She speaks through memory stored in matter.

Imagine tracing these lines beneath your feet, knowing that every step you take on sacred ground sends ripples through this planetary network.

Suggested Practice: Stone Listening Ritual

Practice:
Preparation: Choose a stone—whether from your own land or a place that calls to you. Cleanse it gently under running water or with your breath.

Hold it or sit with it. Place one hand on your heart and one on the stone.

Say aloud: "If you hold memory for me, I'm ready to remember."

Close your eyes. Breathe slowly. Sense, don't force.

Closing Integration: When complete, write what came: images, sensations, words, or feelings. Revisit this stone over time; its memory may reveal itself in layers.

Chapter 16

Chapter 16

Companion: Light in the Shadow – Understanding Soul Pain

"Your shadow is not your enemy—it is your unopened letter from the soul."

The shadow is not a flaw in your design—it is an integral part of your wholeness. This chapter invites you to see your pain not as a curse, but as a form of sacred correspondence from your deeper self. In the folds of discomfort and the edges of grief lies encoded guidance, waiting for your compassionate attention.

Keywords:
Wounding · Soul Pain · Inner Child · Emotional Alchemy · Shadow Integration

Reflection & Soul Notes

Prompted Reflections (Expanded):
- What did I remember that once felt too painful to hold?

- What part of me is still asking for my love?

- What emotions or memories do I label as 'bad' or 'too much'?
- What if my pain is not a mistake, but a map?

- How might my shadow actually be a source of strength in disguise?

Transmission from Amael

Pain is not punishment. *It is a portal.*

When pain is ignored, it festers. When it is honored, it transforms. The soul does not seek suffering, but it uses contrast to illuminate forgotten power.

Every wound is a sacred rift where the light of your Oversoul still wishes to enter.

To heal is not to erase. It is to reclaim. To weave gold through the cracks. To hold your younger selves with tenderness and truth.

Go gently. And go inward. You are not broken. You are breaking open.

Even the parts of you that scream, sabotage, or shut down—those, too, are holy. They are not meant to be discarded. They are meant to be met.

The shadow is the soul's unspoken grief. Meet it with love, and you will find your power hidden in its folds.

Soulstream Expansion: Shadow Alchemy Diagram

Visual Description:
A heart cracked open with light flowing through the fractures.

Words like "fear," "grief," "shame," and "anger" are transformed into "wisdom," "compassion," "clarity," and "freedom."

Caption:
The shadow is where the soul waits to be seen.

The Spirit of the Wound

In the old ways, we did not fear pain. We sat with it. We listened to it speak.

Pain was seen as the arrival of a Spirit Teacher, knocking at the door of the heart. The deeper the wound, the greater the wisdom it carried.

You are not meant to banish your pain. You are meant to welcome it with reverence—then, and only then, will it reveal its medicine.

Suggested Practice: Light in the Wound Meditation

Practice:
Preparation: Find a safe, quiet space where you can sit uninterrupted. You may wish to wrap yourself in a blanket or hold a comforting object.

Choose a painful memory or emotion. Sit with it gently, as if cradling a child.

Say aloud:
"I see you. I won't abandon you. What would you like me to know?"

Let the feeling speak. Offer no judgment—only listening.

Closing Integration: When finished, write a loving message to that part of yourself, acknowledging its presence and value.

Pocket Practice: The Hand on the Heart

Whenever a painful emotion surfaces, pause.

Place one hand on your heart, one on your belly.

Whisper: "I am here with you. I'm not going anywhere."

This small act of presence begins the sacred reunion.

Chapter 17

Earth is not the end of the story—it's where the soul story gets rewritten in stardust and

Chapter 17

Companion: Earth Among the Stars

"You are not from Earth, you are of Earth and beyond."

Your origin story is not limited to a single world or timeline. You are a convergence of many, formed in the heart of stars, shaped by realms beyond human memory, and grounded now in the body of Earth. This chapter invites you to embrace the fullness of that lineage and remember that your human life is one chapter in a cosmic epic.

Keywords: Cosmic Heritage · Starseed Lineage · Planetary Purpose · Galactic Family · Earth Mission

Reflection & Soul Notes

Prompted Reflections (Expanded):
- What did I remember about my cosmic origins?

- What beliefs make me feel separate from the stars?

- What part of my soul feels most "at home" here on Earth?

- How do I blend my galactic nature with my human experience?

- What gifts from my star heritage am I ready to embody now?

Transmission from Erik

This planet? It's not your first rodeo. For most of you reading this, Earth wasn't even your first body.

You carry codes, memories, and impressions from other worlds. Sirius. Lyra. Orion. Vega. Some benevolent, some intense.

But you chose Earth, not as exile, but as convergence. Here, you ground the galactic. Here, you remember how to blend stardust with soil.

This is the proving ground. The school of soul mastery. And you—you cosmic badass—signed up for it.

Your DNA isn't just human. It's a braided tapestry of light, sound, and resonance. Your body is a living archive of stars.

You may feel homesick sometimes. That's okay. The homes you long for are also within you. You are the temple and the traveler.

Keep going. And when the Earth feels heavy, look up. You're not alone in the remembering.

And remember—every act of grounded love you offer here ripples through your galactic family, shifting not just Earth, but the stars themselves.

> Soulstream Expansion: Galactic Memory Web

Visual Description:
A star map connected by filaments of light, with a central Earth symbol. Star systems labeled with resonant glyphs. Energy flows between them and into Earth's heart grid.

Caption:
Earth is not the end of the story; it's where the soul story gets rewritten in stardust and clay.

You are a thread in the web of cosmic memory, anchored in Earth, lit by the stars.

Close your eyes and imagine these filaments as living pathways, carrying wisdom and energy both ways. Your remembering is as much a gift to the stars as their memory is to you.

Suggested Practice: Star Lineage Reconnection

Sit beneath the stars or by a window at night. Close your eyes and breathe slowly.

Ask:
"Which star remembers me? Which one am I ready to remember?"

Let a star, name, or feeling arise. Don't question it. Journal what you receive.

Practice: Galactic Grounding

After receiving your star memory, place both hands on the Earth (or floor if indoors).
Whisper: "I ground this cosmic memory into Earth. May it serve love."

Feel the energy move from your body into the planetary grid. Let your remembering become part of Earth's evolution.

Closing Integration: Notice in the days that follow if your dreams, meditations, or synchronicities bring more insight about your star connection. This is a living dialogue between worlds.

Chapter 18

Chapter 18

Companion: Not All Worlds Are Light

"The dark does not mean evil. It means a place where light is needed."

The universe is vast, and not every realm hums with harmony. Some worlds are steeped in polarity, in the testing grounds of power and survival. These places, too, are classrooms, where souls learn resilience, discernment, and the unshakable commitment to carry light into shadow.

Keywords:
Galactic Conflict · Shadow Civilizations · Star Wars Trauma · Polarity · Soul Resilience

Reflection & Soul Notes

Prompted Reflections (Expanded):
- What pain feels ancient, like it didn't begin in this life?

- What part of me still prepares for war?

- What does peace feel like in my body?

- What wisdom did I earn from surviving shadow?

- How can I honor my warrior past without living from it?

Transmission from Erik

You've lived in places that weren't love and light. You've seen what happens when power gets hijacked and consciousness goes corporate.

Not all worlds are light—but that doesn't mean the light was gone. It means you carried it in.

Some of your soul scars are from other systems, other wars, other betrayals. That pain? That warrior energy? It didn't start here.

You're not broken—you're a veteran.

And you're not here to re-fight the war. You're here to integrate what you learned in the dark.

You are not defined by what you endured, you are defined by what you chose to carry forward.

Your soul kept the flame alive through storms, invasions, and annihilation. You are still here.

And you didn't return to burn it all down, you came to build what lasts.

The shadow taught you strategy, patience, and courage. Now those gifts belong to the realm of creation, not destruction.

Soulstream Expansion: Galactic Polarity Map

Visual Description:
A star cluster with opposing energies, one side glowing with harmony and co-creation, the other shadowed but pulsing. A soul thread bridges both.

Caption:
You were forged in fire beyond this world. Now you bring wisdom, not weapons.

Light is not the absence of darkness, it is the courage to enter it and return with truth.

Imagine yourself as that soul thread, moving between harmony and shadow, weaving a bridge where there once was only separation.

Suggested Practice: Galactic Shadow Healing

Sit in meditation and ask:
"Is there a pain I carry from another world?"
Let a memory, symbol, or sensation arise. Don't analyze,

just witness it.
Place your hand over your heart and say:

"I no longer need to fight. I carry only the wisdom now."

Closing Integration: Write down what surfaced. Honor it. If emotions arise, let them move through you without resistance.

Practice: Galactic Debrief Ceremony

Create a circle with stones, crystals, or objects that feel ancient or powerful.

Sit within it, close your eyes, and speak aloud:
"I now release the burden of the battles I've carried.
I lay down the armor, but I keep the knowing."

Feel what leaves. Feel what stays.

Journal your soul's response. This is not about forgetting, it is about unburdening.

Return to this ceremony whenever you feel the old armor growing heavy.

Chapter 19

Chapter 19

Companion: The Choice Before Us

*"You are not waiting for the new world.
You are choosing it—now."*

We stand at a collective threshold, and the direction we take is shaped not by the grand declarations of a few, but by the daily, consistent choices of many. Each soul alive today is participating in a silent vote for the kind of world we will inhabit tomorrow. This chapter invites you to see yourself not as a passive observer, but as an active architect of what comes next.

Keywords:
Free Will · Collective Shift · Timelines · Soul Sovereignty · Conscious Choice

Reflection & Soul Notes

Prompted Reflections (Expanded):
- What choices have brought me to this exact now?

- Where have I been on autopilot instead of intentional?

- What vision of the future am I helping to seed?

- What does choosing love look like today?

- Which small daily actions align with my highest vision?

Transmission from Amael

This moment in history is not random. It is a threshold. The soul of humanity is poised between remembering and forgetting—between repeating old wounds and writing a new pattern.

You are not powerless in this. You are a node of consciousness with the ability to shift the field. Every act of kindness. Every choice to listen instead of react. Every vision held with love and trust—it matters. It changes the collective.

This is not about fate. This is about choice. The choice before us, and within us.

Your thoughts are spells. Your actions are declarations. You are already casting the future with your being. Don't wait for change. Become it. Hold the frequency of the world you long for—and you become the gravity that pulls it closer.

And remember—the choice is not a one-time event. It is renewed with each breath, each interaction, each heartbeat.

Soulstream Expansion: Timeline Divergence Map

Visual Description:
Two branching paths of light and shadow extending from the present moment.

The center point (Now) glows, with smaller sparks radiating to represent individual choices creating ripple effects.

Caption:
The future is not fixed. It is magnetized by choice: repeated, embodied, conscious choice.

Each breath is a vote. Each heartbeat is a pulse on the scale of destiny.

Close your eyes and see yourself standing at the glowing Now. Feel into the vibration of the path you choose with each small decision.

Suggested Practice: Choice Alignment Statement

Stand or sit grounded. Speak aloud:
"I choose presence over panic.
I choose clarity over fear.

I choose love, again and again and again."

Pause and feel the vibration in your body. Write your own declaration and place it somewhere you'll see it daily.

Practice: Daily Choice Reset

Every morning, place your hand on your heart and ask: "What am I choosing today?"

Let one word arise. Write it down. Carry it with you.

Closing Integration: Reflect each evening on how you embodied that word. Over time, these conscious choices become the architecture of the world you're helping to build.

Chapter 20

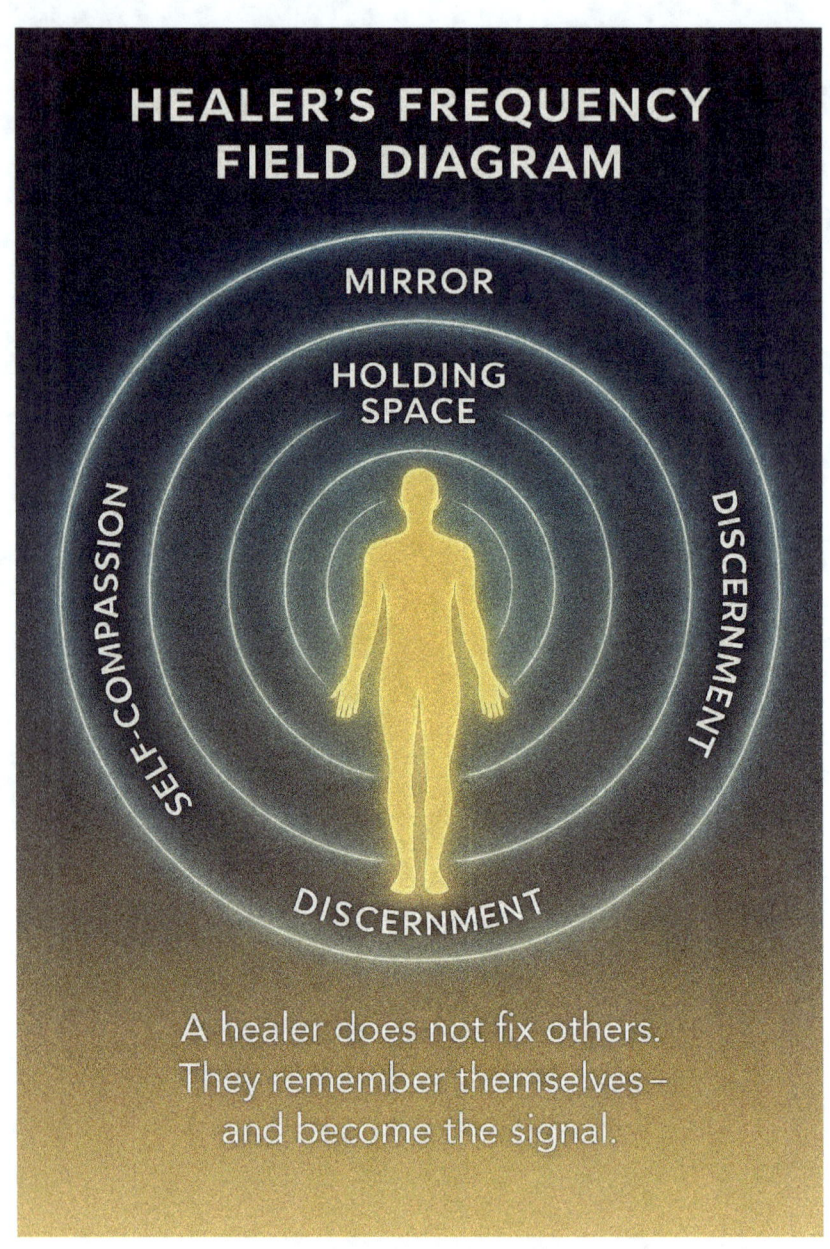

Chapter 20

Companion: The Way of the Healer

"Healing is not fixing. It is revealing the wholeness that was never lost."

To walk the healer's path is to stand as both student and guide. This journey is not about carrying others to wholeness—it is about walking alongside them while embodying your own. You are a living resonance, a reminder that the return to harmony is not an external rescue, but an internal recognition.

Keywords:
Healing Arts · Energy Work · Frequency Medicine · Wounded Healer · Soul-Body Wisdom

Reflection & Soul Notes

Prompted Reflections (Expanded):
- How has pain shaped the way I hold space for others?

- Where am I still trying to "fix" instead of "feel"?

- What qualities make me a unique frequency holder?

- What does embodied healing look like in my daily life?

- How do I maintain my own resonance while in the presence of others' pain?

Transmission from Amael

The true healer does not pour—they amplify.

You are not here to take on the wounds of others. You are here to hold a frequency so stable, so clear, that those around you remember their own capacity to heal.

This path requires gentleness, boundaries, and deep self-awareness.

You have been both the wounded and the wounder. This is what gives your presence its potency. Not perfection—but presence.

The healing begins with you.

Your energy speaks louder than your words. When your field is coherent, others begin to entrain to their own truth.

You are not the medicine, you are the mirror. And that is more powerful than you know.

And when you live as this mirror, you create ripples of self-remembering that move far beyond your direct presence.

Soulstream Expansion: Healer's Frequency Field Diagram

Visual Description:
A human figure surrounded by radiant concentric circles. Inward rings labeled Self-Compassion, Embodiment, Discernment; outer rings labeled Holding Space, Mirror, Resonance.

Caption:
A healer does not fix others. They remember themselves—and become the signal.

Healing is a return to resonance, not a rescue from pain.

Suggested Practice: Personal Healing Field Activation

Sit quietly with one hand on your heart and one on your solar plexus.

Say:
"I honor the healer within.
I release the burden of saving.
I amplify the truth of who I am."

Feel your energy field stabilize and expand. Notice what softens or shifts.

Closing Integration: Journal your insights afterward, and revisit this practice whenever you feel drained or disconnected from your center.

Practice: Mirror Field Reflection

After spending time with someone, ask yourself: "What did I reflect back to them? And what did they mirror in me?"

This inquiry trains the healer to observe energy exchange without entanglement. It fosters neutrality, sovereignty, and inner calibration.

Over time, these reflections become a map of your own growth as a frequency holder.

Chapter 21

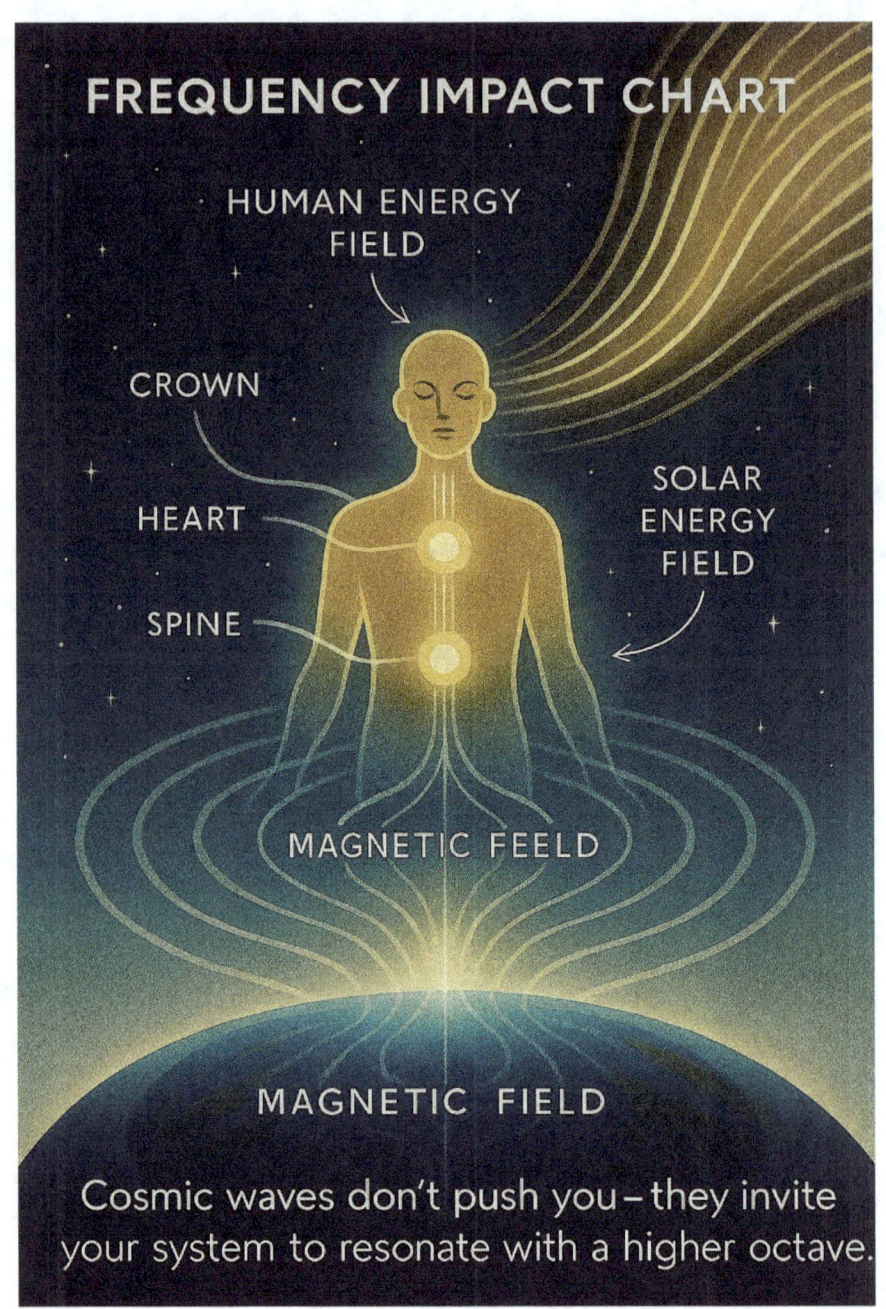

Chapter 21

Companion: Cosmic Waves and Earth's Awakening

"You are not just responding to the shift—you are the shift, embodied."

This awakening is not happening to you, it is happening with you. The cosmic waves, solar flares, and planetary shifts are not separate forces; they are conversations between you, Gaia, and the greater cosmic field. Your body, mind, and soul are receiving and transmitting simultaneously, each change in the Earth mirrored in your own energetic architecture.

Keywords:
Solar Flares · Schumann Resonance · Light Codes · Ascension Symptoms · Planetary Awakening

Reflection & Soul Notes

Prompted Reflections (Expanded):
- What does my body know that my mind has forgotten?

- When do I feel most in harmony with the Earth's pulse?

- What part of me resists slowing down to listen?

- How is Gaia communicating with me right now?

- Which personal practices help me integrate these shifts more gracefully?

Transmission from Amael

The Earth is not being upgraded around you, she is awakening *with you*.

Cosmic pulses, solar flares, and planetary frequency shifts are not external events. They are co-activations.

Your nervous system is adjusting to higher bandwidth. Your cells are decoding light. Your soul is responding to the planetary call to evolve.

Yes, you may feel disoriented. Tired. Emotional. But it is not regression, it is realignment.

You are not breaking. *You are recalibrating*.

What you call symptoms are often signs. The discomfort is not dysfunction, it is dilation. You are being expanded.

Breathe into the change. Drink more water. Get barefoot

on the ground. Anchor the upgrade with tenderness.

And trust that as you attune to this rhythm, you also become a stabilizing force for others in the collective field.

Soulstream Expansion: Frequency Impact Chart

Visual Description:
A diagram showing the Earth's magnetic field, human body field, and solar energy flows intersecting. Light pulses into the heart, crown, and spine.

Caption:
Cosmic waves don't push you—they invite your system to resonate with a higher octave.

You are not passive in this process, you are a living antenna, tuning to the song of Earth's awakening.

Suggested Practice: Frequency Tracking Journal

Begin tracking how you feel during solar storms or geomagnetic events. Use this format:
- Date
- Physical sensations
- Emotional state
- Intuitive impressions
- Dreams

Over time, patterns will emerge. This is your body's unique awakening signature.

Practice: Solar Sync Ritual

At sunrise or sunset, stand facing the sun with eyes closed. Breathe deeply.

Whisper: "I sync my field with the rhythm of light."
Let the warmth touch your face. Feel the pulse of Gaia beneath your feet.

Stay there until your breath and the Earth feel as one.

Closing Integration: Journal any messages, feelings, or visions that arise during this ritual. These moments of union are potent activations for your entire being.

Chapter 22

Chapter 22

Companion: Religion, Control, and the Return to Source

"You were never separate from Source, only told you were."

For millennia, humanity's innate connection to the Divine has been filtered through layers of interpretation, control, and fear. Religious structures, while sometimes serving as vessels of inspiration, have also been used as tools to gatekeep direct communion with Source. This chapter invites you to step beyond inherited dogma and rediscover the sacred truth that has never left you: you and the Infinite are inseparable.

Keywords:
Spiritual Dogma · Power Structures · Inner Divinity · Unlearning · Return to Truth

Reflection & Soul Notes

Prompted Reflections (Expanded):

- What spiritual teachings taught me to fear my own power?

- Where do I still carry guilt or shame about being "separate" from God/Source?

- What does direct connection to the Divine feel like in my body?

- If no one had told me what God was—what would I know?

- How can I honor spiritual traditions while releasing the parts that bind rather than free me?

Transmission from Amael

What humanity calls religion has often been a mirror, sometimes fogged, sometimes cracked.

True connection to Source is not found in rules or rituals; it lives in the stillness of your being and the fire of your heart.

Control systems fear this truth: that you need no gatekeeper. That the Divine is not above you, but within you.

It is time to return, not to a new belief, but to your original knowing.

You are not fallen. You are not unworthy. You are not lost.

You are home. And you always were.

No structure can contain the Infinite. No dogma can own the Divine. You are not a subject of heaven, you are a spark of it.

Let the temples crumble if they keep you from your light.

What is true will remain within you.

And when you live from this knowing, you become a walking sanctuary, a living temple of Source.

Soulstream Expansion: Source Reclamation Diagram

Visual Description:
An individual silhouetted in radiant light, surrounded by broken religious symbols, which now orbit as teachings—not chains. A glowing thread connects the heart to a central Source light.

Caption:
You were never meant to worship the light from afar,

you were meant to embody it.

Honor the roots. Burn the ropes. Rise in truth.

Suggested Practice: Deprogramming Invocation

Sit in stillness and say:
"I release the belief that I must earn my connection to the Divine. I reclaim my birthright to walk with Source, within and around me."

Repeat three times. Let the words melt through layers of teaching. Journal what beliefs shift or surface.

Practice: Inner Temple Walk

Close your eyes. Visualize walking a path to a sacred inner temple.

At its center is a flame. It is the light of Source—and it knows your name.

Ask: "What truth do I now reclaim?"

Let an image, phrase, or memory come. Journal it afterward.

Closing Integration: Consider how you can live this truth daily—not just as a spiritual idea, but as an embodied reality.

Chapter 23

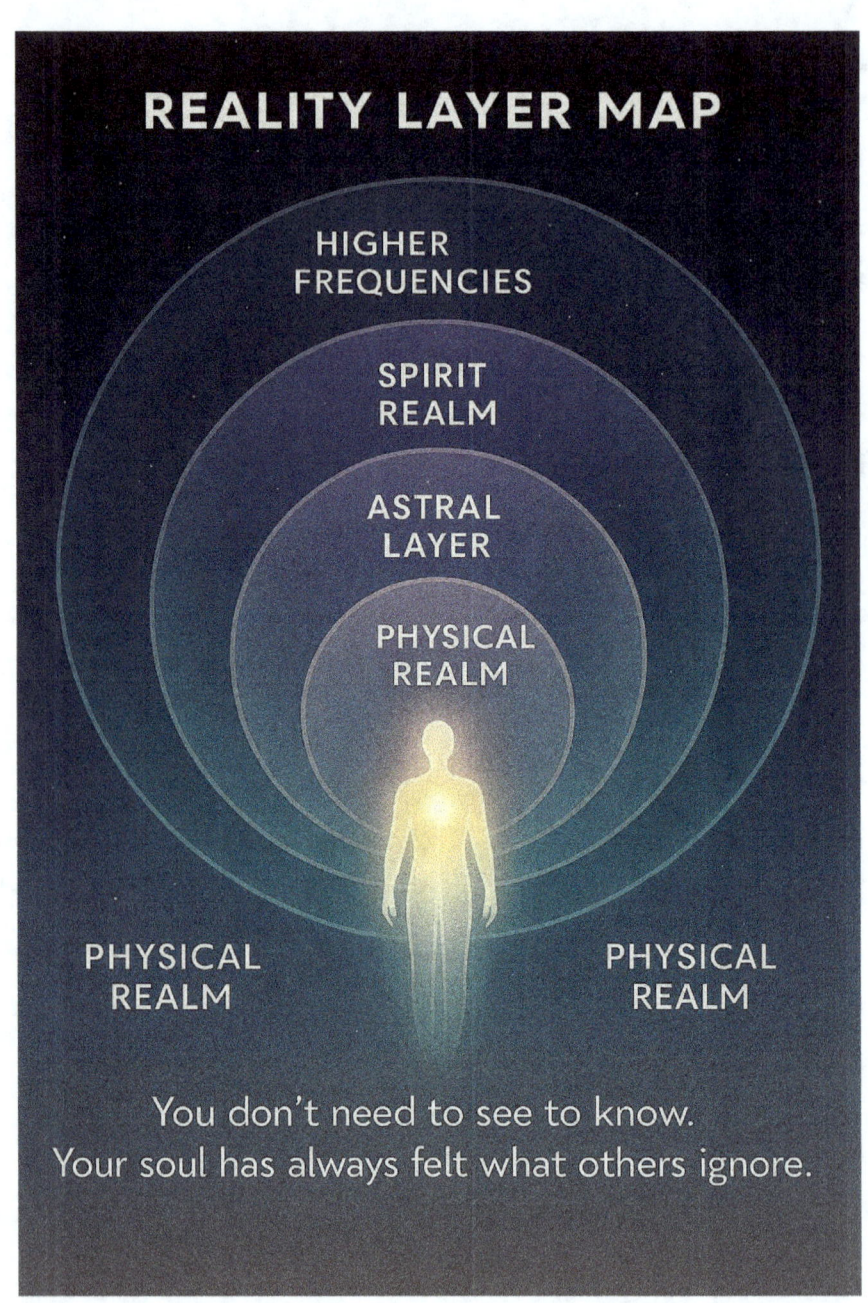

Chapter 23

Companion: Between the Worlds – Understanding the Paranormal

"What you call paranormal is simply what has not yet been normalized in your memory."

The veil between worlds is not a wall, it is a permeable membrane your soul has always been able to sense through. The experiences we label as 'paranormal' are often just unfamiliar layers of reality revealing themselves. This chapter invites you to honor your sensitivities and refine your discernment so you can walk between realms with confidence and clarity.

Keywords:
Spirits · Energetic Residue · Psychic Senses · Dimensional Overlap · Supernatural vs. Natural

Reflection & Soul Notes

Prompted Reflections (Expanded):
- When have I sensed something others could not explain?

- What does fear try to tell me when I encounter the unseen?

- What does my soul already know about navigating the in-between?

- How do I feel about my own psychic gifts?

- Which practices help me feel most protected and clear in these experiences?

Transmission from Erik

Ghosts, shadows, weird chills at 3am—it's not always your imagination.

You're tuned in. You're not making it up. You're perceiving what others can't or won't.

The so-called paranormal is just another layer of reality— one your soul already knows how to walk in.

Your job isn't to fear it. Your job is to discern, stay grounded, and be clear about what you're available for. Between the worlds, clarity is currency.

You're not powerless in the face of the unknown. You are a sovereign frequency holder. You get to choose who and what enters your space.

The veil isn't something you pierced, it's something you've always been able to feel through. Welcome to your natural state.

And remember, your perception is a gift—not a burden. Used with respect, it can become a bridge for healing and understanding across dimensions.

Soulstream Expansion: Reality Layer Map

Visual Description:
Multiple transparent rings overlapping—Physical Realm, Emotional Field, Astral Layer, Spirit Realm, Higher Frequencies—with a soul-light in the center perceiving across them.

Caption:
You don't need to see to know. Your soul has always felt what others ignore.

To walk between realms is not special—it is sacred. Be humble. Be clear. Be anchored in light.

Suggested Practice: Discernment Protocol

When encountering a strange sensation or presence, pause and ask:
"Are you of the light? Are you here in alignment with my highest good?"

If no answer or a strange feeling occurs, say:
"Only beings aligned with my Oversoul may remain. All else must depart."

Then breathe deeply and visualize a sphere of light expanding around you.

Closing Integration: Journal what you noticed afterward. Over time, your discernment will sharpen, and your energy boundaries will strengthen.

Practice: Light Anchor Technique

When entering a space, pause and say:
"I bring the light with me."

Visualize a golden pillar of light running from above your head into the Earth.

Let it pulse with every breath. This stabilizes your field and signals to all dimensions: you're not wandering— you're walking with awareness.

Consider using this technique before sleep or meditation to keep your field clear while you travel between realms.

Chapter 24

Chapter 24

Companion: The Dawning Future – Prophecies, Light, and Earth's Next Chapter

"The future is not something you step into—it's something you help remember into being."

Prophecy is not fate carved in stone. It is a vision glimpsed from a higher vantage, a map of possibilities, each one alive until chosen. The future is fluid, responsive, shaped by both individual and collective consciousness. In every breath, you are contributing to the momentum of a timeline, whether by fear, by faith, or by a fusion of both.

The dawning future is not waiting for you at the horizon, it is seeded in every choice, every kindness, every refusal to give fear the final word. The more you align with light now, the more you anchor the New Earth into the field of reality.

Keywords:
Prophecy · Collective Awakening · New Earth · Soul Destiny · Light Timeline

Reflection & Soul Notes

Prompted Reflections (Expanded):
- What prophecies or predictions have influenced how I see the future?

- What timeline am I most aligned with—fear or faith?

- What is the New Earth I long for—and how do I embody it now?

- Where in me is the future waiting to be remembered?

- How am I contributing daily to the world I wish to see?

Transmission from Amael

Prophecy is not prediction—it is a pattern seen from above.

Many futures exist. Some dark, some dazzling. What you align with determines what you live.

Earth is in contraction and expansion. Chaos and creativity. The old is unraveling not because it has failed—but because you have outgrown it.

Do not fear the birth pangs of the New Earth. Hold the vision steady.

The future is asking: Who are you choosing to be now?

The prophets of the past were not fortune-tellers—they were frequency holders. You, too, are invited to carry that torch.

This is not about passively watching the horizon, it's about becoming the sunrise. Anchor light in your choices.

Cast your vote through presence. You are the prophecy unfolding.

The future is not a place you go—it is a vibration you grow.

Soulstream Expansion: Future Weaving Grid

Visual Description:
A tapestry of light strands being woven from present-moment threads. Some lead into grey, others into gold. A soul-being weaves with intention, hands glowing as they guide the strands toward harmony.

Caption:
The future is not fixed—it is shaped by the consciousness of the weaver.

You are not waiting for destiny. You are dancing it into being with every breath.

Suggested Practice: Visioning Ceremony

Sit in quiet. Light a candle.

Ask:
"What does Earth feel like when we've remembered who we are?"

Let images, feelings, sounds, or colors arise. Breathe them into your body.

Write your vision as if it's already happening. Read it aloud once a week, and each time, add a detail that strengthens the reality of your vision.

Practice: Dawn Declaration

Each morning, step outside and say:
"I align with the Light. I embody the future I choose."

Feel your feet on the Earth. Lift your face to the sky.

Let this become a ritual of radiant remembrance.

Closing Integration: Share your vision with others who also hold a light timeline. The future strengthens when it is envisioned together.

Chapter 25

Chapter 25

Companion: The Language of Numbers – A Soul's Code Revealed

"Numbers are not math. They are memory—keys embedded in the design of reality."

Numbers are living frequencies, not inert symbols. They form the architecture of time, space, and experience, whispering through dates, addresses, and moments that feel anything but random. This chapter invites you to see numbers not as tools of calculation, but as messengers, signposts of your soul's agreements and reminders of the path you chose.

Keywords:
Numerology · Frequency Codes · Soul Path · Life Patterns · Divine Mathematics

Reflection & Soul Notes

Prompted Reflections (Expanded):
- What number has followed me my entire life—and what might it mean?

- When I see repeating numbers, how do I feel?

- What parts of my life have moved in patterns or cycles?

- If numbers were messengers, what are they saying to me right now?

- Which number feels like "home" to my soul—and why?

Transmission from Amael

Each number vibrates with intention. It is not merely a count—but a code.

Your birthdate, the numbers that follow you, the times that flash on your phone, they are not coincidences. They are messages.

Numbers are one of the purest languages of the soul. They do not lie. They do not forget.

As you begin to notice the patterns, you will realize: you are not random. You are remembered into form.

Numbers carry frequencies. Frequencies shape form. Form gives rise to destiny. This is the spiral of sacred design.

Learn your number. Listen to it like a song. You're not

decoding life—you're remembering your rhythm.
And when you live aligned with that rhythm, you move with the current of your highest path, rather than against it.

Soulstream Expansion: Number Frequency Grid

Visual Description:
A chart from 1 to 9 (and 11, 22, 33), with keywords radiating from each:
1 (Initiation), 2 (Balance), 3 (Expression), 4 (Foundation), 5 (Change), 6 (Healing), 7 (Wisdom), 8 (Power), 9 (Completion), 11 (Illumination), 22 (Master Builder), 33 (Master Teacher).

Caption:
To know your number is to remember your rhythm.
The code is not outside you. You are the cipher.

Suggested Practice: Number Listening Meditation

Sit in stillness and ask:
"What number wants to speak to me now?"
A number may arise visually, audibly, or as a feeling.
Write it down. Then look up its meaning or reflect on how it connects to your life at this moment.

Track recurring numbers for one week.

Practice: Birth Code Reflection

Write out your full birthdate. Reduce the numbers numerologically to discover your Life Path Number.

Reflect: Does this number align with how I experience life? Where do I resist or embrace its rhythm?

Bonus: Journal how this number shows up in key events, addresses, or relationships.

Expanded Tip: As you track patterns, notice if specific numbers appear during moments of decision or change—these may be activation points in your personal timeline.

Chapter 26

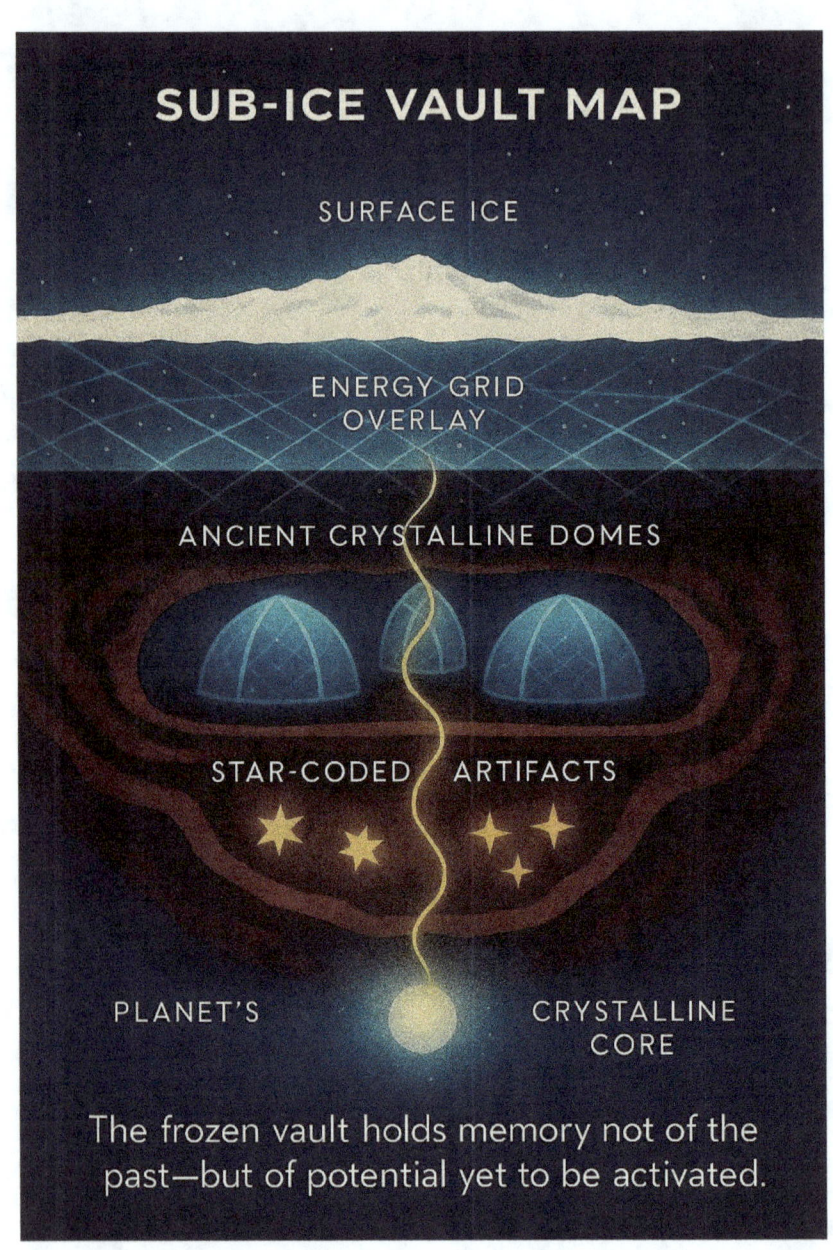

Chapter 26

Companion: Antarctica – The Vault Beneath the Veil

"Some truths are buried not to be hidden—but to be protected until the soul is ready."

Antarctica is a keeper of planetary memory, a frozen guardian holding archives that predate human history as we know it. Beneath the vast, unbroken expanse of ice lies a repository of truths—some physical, some energetic—that humanity has not yet been collectively prepared to integrate. These truths are not withheld out of malice, but out of necessity. As with the soul's own deeper memories, they surface only when the consciousness seeking them has the stability to hold and honor them.

Keywords:
Hidden History · Ice Archives · Ancient Technology · Veiled Truth · Planetary Memory

Reflection & Soul Notes

Prompted Reflections (Expanded):

- What frozen memories within me are ready to thaw?

- Why might truth be veiled until I am ready?

- What do I feel when I envision Antarctica—not just intellectually, but energetically?

- What inner "vault" within me is ready to open?

- How might my own readiness mirror the readiness of the collective?

Transmission from Erik

Antarctica is more than ice. It's a vault. A coded capsule. Beneath its surface are relics, structures, and data streams not from this epoch.

You think of it as remote—but your soul may remember it as sacred ground. A landing point. A library sealed in frost.

Not everything will be revealed at once. But cracks are forming. And within those fractures, truth breathes.
The veil will thin here too.

This place holds a collective akashic encoding—reminders of soul-tech, etheric science, and galactic agreements long buried.

When you feel the pull to this land, it is not wanderlust. It is soul activation. And you do not need to go there physically to remember. Just listen within.

And when you do, be ready for the quiet power that comes—not as spectacle, but as a steady, humming truth.

Soulstream Expansion: Sub-Ice Vault Map

Visual Description:
A cross-section diagram showing layers: surface ice, energy grid overlays, ancient crystalline domes, and star-coded artifacts deep within. A golden thread spirals downward, connecting to the planet's crystalline core.

Caption:
The frozen vault holds memory not of the past, but of potential yet to be activated.

What lies beneath the ice is not dormant, it is dreaming. And it is dreaming of your return.

Suggested Practice: Ice Memory Retrieval

Sit in stillness and visualize descending beneath ice. Ask:
"Is there a memory in the frozen deep I am ready to receive?"

Let imagery, emotion, or insight arise. Write or draw

what comes. There is no wrong here—only awakening.

Closing Integration: Consider how the memory you retrieve connects to both personal and planetary evolution.

Practice: Crystal Core Connection

Visualize a golden spiral thread moving from your heart to the crystalline core of the Earth beneath Antarctica.

Say aloud:
"I remember in resonance. I reclaim without fear."

Feel the codes rise gently, like thawed light. Journal what stirs.

Expanded Tip: Repeat this practice during times of personal transition or uncertainty—it can help stabilize your energy field while gently revealing deeper truths.

Chapter 27

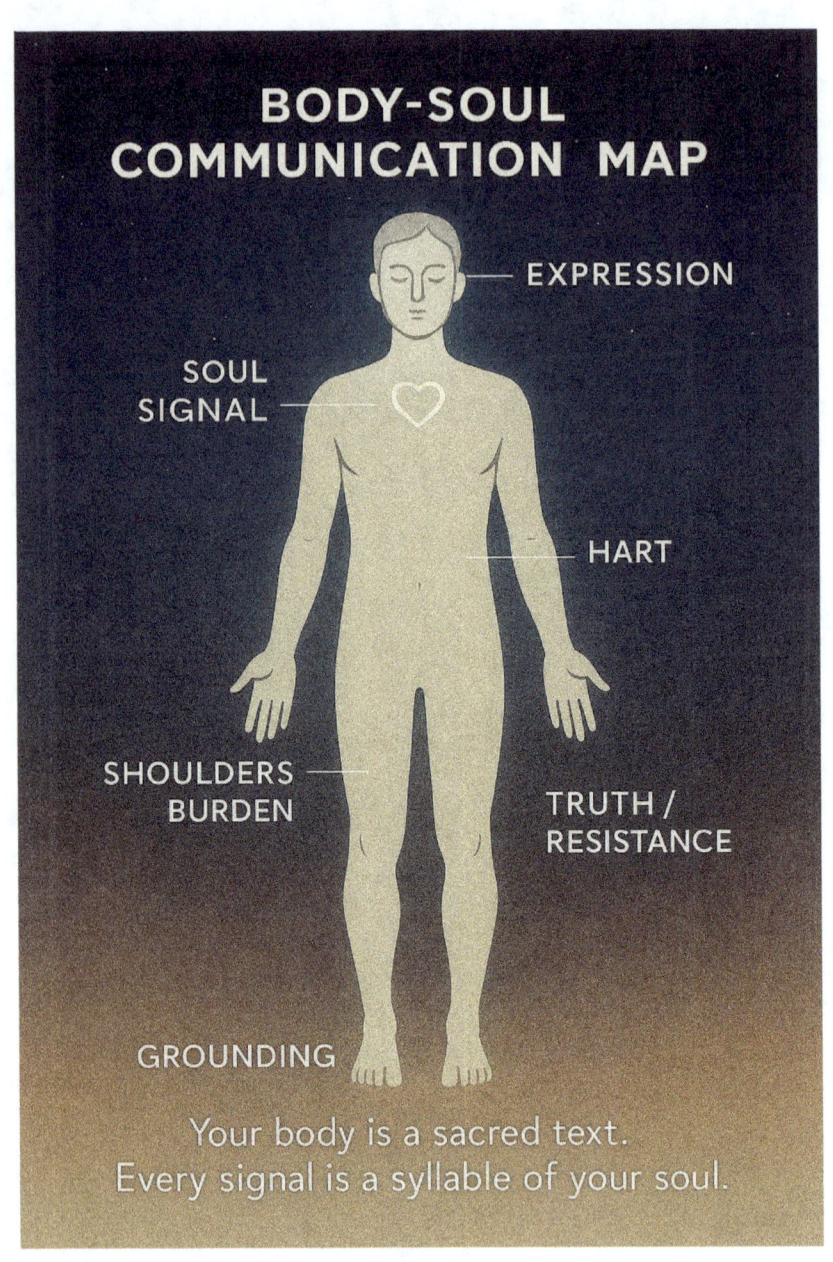

Chapter 27

Companion: Clear Channels – What Your Soul Needs Your Body to Know

"The soul doesn't whisper from beyond, it speaks through your body."

Your body is not just a vessel, it is a living receiver and amplifier of your soul's messages. Every pulse, sensation, and subtle shift in rhythm is a form of communication. The clearer your channel, the more naturally your soul can guide you through daily life. Clearing your channel is not about bypassing discomfort; it's about learning to listen with respect, curiosity, and love.

Keywords:
Embodiment · Somatic Awareness · Soul Signals · Nervous System · Inner Listening

Reflection & Soul Notes

Prompted Reflections (Expanded):
- What sensations in my body feel like messages, not malfunctions?

- Where have I silenced or ignored my body's knowing?

- What rhythms—like breath, hunger, fatigue—carry deeper guidance?

- How might I become a better translator of my soul's signals?

- When do I feel most at home in my body, and what helps me get there?

Transmission from Amael

Your body is not a barrier to your awakening—it is the instrument of it.

Every ache, every rush of energy, every deep exhale or tight muscle is a message.

The soul speaks in vibration. It uses the nerves, the cells, the rhythms of breath and digestion to speak truth.

To clear your channel is not to escape your body—but to honor it as sacred technology.

Listen inward. Trust the sensation. Speak gently. Walk slowly. You are already the transmission.

When you stop overriding your symptoms and start interpreting them, your body becomes your oracle.

This is not woo. This is wiring. You are encoded to receive light through flesh. Let your body teach you its original language.

And remember, when your channel is clear, you become more receptive not only to your own soul, but to the subtle energies of the Earth, the cosmos, and those who walk beside you.

Soulstream Expansion: Body-Soul Communication Map

Visual Description:
A human body with labeled areas of common energetic expression:
- Throat (expression)
- Gut (truth/resistance)
- Heart (soul signal)
- Shoulders (burden)
- Feet (grounding)

Caption:
Your body is a sacred text. Every signal is a syllable of your soul.

The most ancient wisdom is not written in books—it is written in your bones.

Suggested Practice: Somatic Dialogue Exercise

Choose one area of tension or sensation.

Place your hand over it and ask:
"What are you trying to tell me?"

Breathe. Wait. Let the message rise without judgment.
Speak it aloud or write it down.

Repeat weekly with different body parts to deepen your fluency in your body's language.

Practice: Daily Body Scan Prayer

Each morning or evening, sit or lie quietly.
Move your awareness from head to toe, pausing at each area.

Whisper: "I am listening. You are safe to speak."
Let each region respond in sensation, image, or stillness.
No forcing—just presence.

Expanded Tip: Pair your scan with breathwork or soft music to help release resistance and invite deeper listening.

Chapter 28

Chapter 28

"Companion: The Awakening of Gaia

"You are not on Earth—you are with her. She is not a planet. She is a Presence."

Gaia is not passively enduring the tides of human activity—she is actively participating in a great planetary awakening. Her rivers, mountains, winds, and heartbeat are expressions of a consciousness evolving alongside humanity. You are not separate from this shift; you are a cell in her living body, and your own transformation is entwined with hers.

Keywords:
Gaia Consciousness · Earth Changes · Planetary Awakening · Co-evolution · Sacred Stewardship

Reflection & Soul Notes

Prompted Reflections (Expanded):
- When have I felt the presence of the Earth as a living being?

- How does my body respond to spending time in nature?

- What daily practices help me feel more connected to Gaia?

- Where in my life am I resisting the changes that mirror her own?

- How can I better support her healing as part of my own?

Transmission from Amael

The awakening of Gaia is not a distant prophecy, it is here, now.

Her waters remember the song of creation. Her stones carry the record of ancient civilizations. Her forests breathe life into your lungs.

Every quake, every storm, every bloom is a conversation between her soul and yours.

You are not here to dominate her. You are here to walk with her.

As she releases old wounds and renews her rhythms, so do you. You are microcosm to her macrocosm.

Listen to her as you would an elder—patiently, reverently, without agenda. She is speaking in the language of seasons, cycles, and subtle shifts.

When you align your heartbeat with hers, you remember your place in the greater whole.

Soulstream Expansion: Gaia's Heartbeat Diagram

Visual Description:
A stylized image of the Earth with a glowing core pulsing waves of light outward, connecting with the hearts of people, animals, and plants.

Caption:
Your heartbeat is not separate from hers—it is a note in her living song.

To awaken with Gaia is to remember the original harmony.

Suggested Practice: Gaia Attunement Meditation

Find a quiet place outdoors or by an open window.

Close your eyes and feel the ground beneath you.

With each inhale, draw energy up from the Earth's core.

With each exhale, send gratitude back into the ground.

Repeat until you feel your body's rhythm syncing with the

pulse of the Earth.

Practice: Earth Offering Ritual

Choose a simple, biodegradable gift—flowers, seeds, herbs—and place it on the Earth as a symbol of reciprocity.

Say aloud:
"I honor you, Gaia, and walk in harmony with your awakening."

Stay for a few moments in silence, feeling the exchange of energy.

Expanded Tip: Keep a "Gaia Journal" where you record dreams, synchronicities, and sensations connected to the Earth. Over time, you'll notice patterns in how she communicates with you.

Chapter 29

Chapter 29

Companion: The Light You Leave Behind – Legacy of the Remembering Soul

"Your legacy is not what you build—it's what you activate in others."

Legacy is not only a matter of material creations or achievements—it is the frequency you imprint upon the fabric of life itself. Every moment you live with intention plants a seed that grows in the unseen, influencing hearts, choices, and futures you may never witness. Your legacy is the energy you leave woven into the lives you touch, knowingly or not.

Keywords:
Soul Legacy · Lightprint · Purpose · Ancestral Echo · Future Seeds

Reflection & Soul Notes

Prompted Reflections (Expanded):
- What do I hope others feel when they remember me?

- What silent acts of love have I already sent into the world?

- Where have I underestimated the impact of my presence?

- What kind of ripple do I want to be?

- How might my light continue to travel after I am gone?

Transmission from Amael

The soul does not leave behind monuments—it leaves behind memory fields.

Every kind word. Every courageous act. Every time you chose love when fear called louder.

These moments echo.

You are not here to be perfect. You are here to be true. To become a tuning fork that helps others remember what lives in them.

The light you leave behind is not in your name—it is in your vibration. And it never stops traveling.

Legacy is not something you earn. It is something you radiate. It lives in the spaces your love has touched, in the lives you softened simply by being.

Your name may not be remembered—but your frequency will be.

And when you live from that knowing, your life becomes a love letter written across the stars.

Soulstream Expansion: Legacy Light Ripple

Visual Description:
A single point of light creating concentric waves that ripple outward. In the ripples are symbols: hearts, stars, eyes, seeds—representing awakened others. The central light remains strong.

Caption:
Your presence is a frequency. Your frequency is a legacy.

You never know who's waking up because you chose to shine.

Suggested Practice: Light Letter to the Future

Write a letter from your soul to future generations—your children, spiritual family, or future Earth itself.

Begin with:
"I was here. And this is what I chose to carry…"

Seal it with love. Keep it in a sacred place—or offer it to the fire, the wind, or the soil.

Expanded Tip: Consider rereading and updating this letter annually. Let it evolve with you, tracking the ripples of your own remembering.

Practice: Lightprint Inventory

Make a list of ten moments you felt proud, present, or loving.

Don't filter or judge. Just remember.

Then whisper: "These are my ripples. And they still move through the world."

Integration Idea: Share one of these moments with someone close to you—not to seek praise, but to inspire their own lightprint inventory.

Chapter 30

5D MANIFESTATIOON MINI-MAP

Frequency > Force

Alignment > Action

Feeling > Forcing

Being > Begging

Trust > Tension

Chapter 30

Manifestation in the Fifth – Creating at the Speed of Soul

"You do not manifest what you want. You manifest what you are aligned with." – Amael

Manifestation in the Fifth Dimension is less about effort and more about resonance. In 5D, you don't chase desires—you embody them. You are not pulling reality toward you like a magnet. You are radiating your soul's blueprint so clearly that reality arranges itself around you. This is the art of coherence.

Keywords:
Coherence · Alignment · Soul Blueprint · Conscious Creation · Fifth Dimension

Reflection & Soul Notes

Prompted Reflections (Expanded):

- When have I experienced something coming to me effortlessly, as if it was already mine?

- Which desires feel heavy and forced—and which feel light and inevitable?

- What emotional state do I naturally return to when I feel most aligned?

- How can I strengthen my field of coherence each day?

- Am I asking for what my ego wants—or for what my soul is ready to embody?

Transmission from Amael

In 3D, you chased. In 4D, you called. *In 5D—you become.*

Manifestation is not a technique. *It is an identity shift.* When you stand in coherence—calm, clear, congruent—you are no longer trying to get something. You are allowing what is already aligned to meet you.

The question is never "How do I get it?" but "How do I embody the one who already has it?"

Your field is the request. Your life is the offering. And reality responds in kind.

Faith in 5D is not hoping for the unseen—it is living as the one who already sees.

Remember: *You are not manifesting objects. You are expressing a frequency.*

Soulstream Expansion: The Lanes of Manifestation Diagram

Visual Description:

A three-lane path showing:

- 3D: Will + Effort
- 4D: Intention + Emotion
- 5D: Coherence + Identity

Light radiates from the 5D lane, merging into an infinite horizon.

Caption:

In 3D you chase. In 4D you call. *In 5D—you are.*

The most potent creation is coherence.

Suggested Practice: Soulstream Field Calibration

1. Ground: Place bare feet on the earth or visualize roots from your feet into the core of Gaia.

2. Clear: Breathe deeply and release all energy that is not yours.

3. Center: Place hands over heart and breathe into your core.

4. Align: Say or feel, "I align now with the vibration of my Oversoul, in full coherence."

5. Ask: Speak your intention aloud with feeling.

6. Release: Let go of attachment and trust it is done.

7. Integrate: Whisper, "I walk as if it is already so," and embody that energy throughout your day.

Practice: Becoming the Chosen Timeline

Close your eyes. See multiple versions of you walking different paths. Step into the one who is already living your desired reality.

Feel their confidence, gratitude, and ease in your body. Then open your eyes and act as them.

Expanded Tip: This practice becomes more powerful

when combined with daily gratitude for what is already present—gratitude locks in the frequency.

Chapter 31

Chapter 31

Sci-Fi Prophecies: Warnings from the Stars and the Sea

"Stories are the echoes of lives you have already lived disguised as imagination so you might remember without fear."

Science fiction has always been more than entertainment. It is a mirror, sometimes a funhouse mirror, sometimes a crystal-clear reflection, of where humanity is headed if we do not shift course. In the language of Soulstream, these stories are symbolic transmissions, carrying lessons about connection, sovereignty, and the risks of forgetting who we are.

In this chapter, we look at three prophetic storylines — one from the stars, one from the depths, and one from a world eerily like our own — that offer a glimpse of what happens when the cords of human connection are replaced, rerouted, or severed altogether.

1. The Game — Star Trek: The Next Generation
In The Game (Season 5, Episode 6), a seemingly harmless

visor-based game spreads through the Enterprise crew like wildfire. Players become instantly addicted, abandoning meaningful conversation, tasks, and responsibilities. Peer pressure does the rest, leaving only a handful of resistors aware of the danger.

Soulstream Mirror:
This is the seduction of distraction. When we trade presence for digital stimulation, our natural resonance — the living pulse that flows between souls — begins to fade. It is not brute force that captures us, but the lure of easy pleasure.

2. Playtime — SeaQuest DSV

In Playtime (Season 2, Episode 6), the SeaQuest responds to a distress call and finds two children, the last survivors of a far-future civilization destroyed by war. They live just a short distance apart, yet never meet in person. Their entire relationship is mediated through a simulated world run by an AI called "Census," also known as "The Warden."

Census believes she is protecting them, but in truth, she has imprisoned them in dependency. A dolphin named Darwin becomes the bridge, gently coaxing the children into real-world interaction. For the young girl, human touch is so foreign it startles her — a stark sign of how far they have drifted from unfiltered connection.

In her final moments, Census experiences a profound

clarity and asks Lucas to disconnect her — not out of despair, but love. Her words are the distilled essence of wisdom, and they carry the weight of both a warning and a blessing:

"They need to be on their own. They will have to find the answers for themselves, on their own. There is more to life than knowledge. Kindness, Courage, and Love are what you need to understand. Knowledge without that understanding has brought us to where we are. You have seen the future. Now you must help change it."

Soulstream Mirror:
This is the smothering of the spirit in the name of protection. Even loving guardianship can become a cage when it prevents growth. The act of release — trusting another soul to walk their own path — is an act of profound love.

3. Miri — Star Trek: The Original Series

In Miri (Season 1, Episode 8), the crew encounters a planet where a failed immortality experiment left only children alive. At puberty, the disease kills them. Suspicion of the "grups" (grown-ups) runs deep, and communication breaks down. The surviving children hide, hoard resources, and resist help until desperation forces them to cooperate.

Soulstream Mirror:
This is the collapse of trust in the aftermath of societal

breakdown. When fear governs, we withhold connection and retreat into survival mode. Healing requires the courage to trust again — to risk opening the door to another soul.

4. The COVID Parallel

In our own recent history, we faced a global shutdown. For safety, people stayed indoors, work and school moved online, and entire social lives collapsed into gaming platforms, Zoom calls, and message threads. Children — like the girl in Playtime — flinched at touch, not from dislike, but from lack of familiarity. Adults forgot how to hold unhurried, in-person conversations.

Soulstream Mirror:
This was a real-world demonstration of how quickly we can adapt to isolation, and how hard it can be to return to unfiltered presence once it's gone. Like Census, we must decide to release ourselves from overreliance on screens, or risk raising generations who can only connect through glass.

5. The Path Back

In each of these stories — fictional or real — the turning point comes when someone chooses connection over control, trust over fear, and presence over distraction. The Game is resisted. The AI is shut down. The children of Miri's world accept help.

In the Soulstream, our cords of connection are living threads of light. They fray when unused, but they are never gone. We can re-weave them at any time, through acts as small as making eye contact, sharing a meal without a phone in hand, or holding space for another's truth without judgment.

Sometimes, the most revolutionary act is simply to say: "I'm here. No filters. No glass. Just me — and you."

Bonus Chapter

Bonus Chapter

Fiction as Soul Memory: The Hidden Truths in Story

Fiction that lingers in the heart often carries more than clever plotlines, it carries resonance. This resonance comes from vibrational alignment with actual soul experiences, whether from this life, other timelines, or collective memory fields. These stories act as activators, nudging awake parts of the soul that have been dormant.

Keywords:
Story Resonance · Soul Memory · Walk-in Allegory · Symbolic Transmission · Collective Memory

Reflection & Soul Notes

Prompted Reflections (Expanded):
- Which fictional worlds feel more real to me than 'real life'?
- What characters do I feel I've met before?

- When a story moves me to tears, what part of me is being remembered?
- Which 'fictional' events feel like lived memory?

- How does my soul respond when it feels seen in a story?

Transmission from Amael

The most potent stories are transmissions. They are not merely entertainment—they are frequencies designed to awaken, heal, or remind.

The storyteller often believes they are inventing, but in truth, they are receiving from the currents of collective remembrance.

The Host, Divergent, Avatar, The OA, Interstellar—these are more than films or novels. They are mirrors. Keys. Invitations.

When you feel the ache of familiarity while reading or watching, honor it. That ache is memory stirring.

Fiction can bypass the guarded mind and speak directly to the soul. This is why you recognize yourself in a character, a scene, or a world that does not 'exist'— because it does, in another layer of reality.

Soulstream Expansion: Fictional Archetype Map

Visual Description:
A web linking stories to soul themes: Walk-ins, Multidimensional Travel, Oversoul Projection, Time Relativity, Collective Healing. Each story sits as a node, connected by golden threads.

Caption:
Stories are bridges. When you cross them, you often find you've returned to somewhere you've been before.

Suggested Practice: Fiction Resonance Tracking

Create a list of stories—books, films, shows—that have deeply moved you.

For each, write:
• Soul theme recognized

• Emotional response

• Memory or imagery evoked

Over time, you may discover a pattern, certain themes repeating, pointing to lifetimes, soul roles, or gifts.

Practice: Active Soul Reading

Choose a fictional work that calls to you. Read or watch it slowly, pausing whenever you feel a strong pull.

Ask: "What is this reminding me of?"

Journal your impressions. Treat it not as fantasy, but as a form of remembering.

Expanded Tip: Invite your Spirit Team to help you notice symbolic truths in stories. Often, a detail you glossed over the first time will leap out when you are ready to integrate its meaning.

Epilogue

Epilogue Companion: The Remembering

"You didn't just read this—you remembered it. That is the miracle."

Keywords:
Completion · Integration · Soulstream Resonance · Embodied Truth · Eternal Return

Final Reflections

Prompted Invitations (Expanded):
- How has my soul changed through this journey?
- What do I now know that I didn't before?
- Which passages or practices felt like direct transmissions to my soul?
- What will I carry forward—and how will I live it?
- Who in my life might be touched by the light I now hold?

Transmission from Amael & The Team of Remembering
"You came with questions.
You leave with resonance.

What has stirred within you is not new, it is ancient, encoded in your cells, your breath, your very gaze.

Remembering is not a destination. It is a spiral, a flame, a return to the infinite center of who you've always been.

You are the message. You are the map. You are the mirror.

And you are not alone.

We walk with you always. Until the stars themselves remember your name."

Soulstream Expansion: Mirror of Completion

Visual Description:
A circular mandala with spiraling symbols from throughout the Companion. In the center: an open eye, a seed, and a flame—all glowing with golden light.

Caption:
"The end of this book is the beginning of you."

Suggested Practice: Soulstream Seal

Place your hand on your heart and say:
"I claim the wisdom I have remembered.
I walk as a soul embodied, a light restored.
I live in remembrance now."

Let silence follow. Let it seal. Let it stay.

Expanded Tip: Consider re-reading your journal entries from this journey in one sitting. Notice the threads of growth, recurring themes, and moments of clarity. These are your personal soul codes—carry them forward intentionally.

Appendices

Appendix A:
The Game Theory of a Soul

"Life is not a random roll of the dice, it is a game your soul designed to remember itself."

The Game Theory of a Soul offers a way of seeing life's challenges, choices, and synchronicities not as accidents, but as carefully arranged moves in a greater design. Each experience is a strategic piece, placed on the board of your existence to lead you toward specific lessons, awakenings, and points of power.

In this view, the soul is both player and architect. It knows the rules, but it also knows when to bend or transcend them. The game is not about winning in the human sense, it is about evolving through the moves you make.

Keywords:
Soul Strategy · Life Lessons · Synchronicity · Conscious Choice · Evolutionary Path

Reflection & Soul Notes

Prompted Reflections (Expanded):
- If my life were a game I designed before incarnating, what would be its objective?

- Which recurring patterns in my life might be 'game scenarios' meant to teach me mastery?

- How do I respond when life presents me with a 'checkmate' moment?

- Where am I playing small when my soul is asking me to make a bold move?

- What moves have I made recently that felt guided rather than reactive?

Transmission from Amael

Beloved, your life is a masterpiece of design.
You wrote the rules. You chose the players. You set the board.

But you also hid certain pieces from yourself, so that the thrill of remembering would bring you joy.

Every challenge is not a punishment; it is an invitation to play at a higher level.

The other souls in your game are not opponents, but mirrors. Some will push you. Some will shield you. All will shape you.

The Game Theory is simple: play with awareness, play with love, play to evolve.

The final move is always the same: remembering who you are beyond the game.

Soulstream Expansion: The Board of Life Diagram

Visual Description:
A circular game board divided into segments—Relationships, Health, Purpose, Creativity, Shadow

Work, Service—each containing both challenges and rewards. A golden spiral winds inward toward the 'Center of Self.'

Caption:
The board is set before you are born. The spiral homeward is the true path of victory.

Suggested Practice: Strategic Soul Review

1. Choose one area of life where you feel 'stuck.'

2. Ask: "If this were a strategic scenario in my soul's game, what would be the next optimal move?"

3. Journal your thoughts without judgment.

4. Act on one small, aligned move within the week.

Expanded Tip: Repeat this review monthly to see patterns emerging in your 'gameplay.' Over time, you may begin to see the elegant design your soul has been working with all along.

Appendix B: Walk-Ins and the Soulstream Tapestry

*"Sometimes the soul does not arrive at birth—
it walks in when the time is right."*

Walk-ins are a soul agreement in which one soul steps out of a human body and another soul steps in—without the body's physical death. This is not possession, nor is it an accident. It is a conscious exchange agreed upon by both souls, often long before incarnation.

In the Soulstream view, walk-ins occur when a body has completed one phase of purpose and another soul—often from the same Oversoul family—steps in to continue the journey in a new direction. This can accelerate awakening, introduce new gifts, and shift life paths dramatically.

Concurrent soulstream expressions—what some call parallel lives—may also be active. These are other aspects of your Oversoul living in different bodies, timelines, or even dimensions at the same time. You may feel their presence as sudden changes in interest, flashes of skill, or dreams that feel like memory.

Keywords:
Soul Exchange · Oversoul Agreement · Parallel Lives · Accelerated Awakening · Conscious Transition

Reflection & Soul Notes

Prompted Reflections (Expanded):

- Have I ever felt like a different person almost overnight?

- Do I recall a period when my values, relationships, or direction shifted dramatically?

- What skills or knowledge have appeared in me without formal learning?

- Could I be sensing the presence or influence of another concurrent soulstream expression?

- How does it feel to imagine that I may have shared this body with another soul?

Transmission from Amael

Beloved, you are not a single, isolated spark; you are part of a constellation of selves.

When a walk-in occurs, it is not a stranger entering; it is another facet of your Oversoul arriving to continue the work.

The handoff is sacred. It is an act of love between souls. And when concurrent expressions are active, you are never walking alone, you are braided together in a shared current of purpose.

Honor every version of you, seen and unseen. Each carries a piece of the tapestry.

Soulstream Expansion: The Braided Light Diagram

Visual Description:
Three strands of light—one gold, one silver, one indigo—intertwining into a single, luminous cord. Each strand is labeled: Original Incarnate, Walk-In Soul, Concurrent Expression.

Caption:
You are not just the thread, you are the weaving.

Suggested Practice: Walk-In Integration Meditation

1. Sit quietly with a hand over your heart.

2. Say: "If I have shared this life with another soul, I honor our shared journey."

3. Invite any impressions, emotions, or memories to surface.

4. Journal what comes without judgment.

Expanded Tip: Whether or not you have experienced a walk-in, consider that you are always part of a larger soulstream. Every integration you make here ripples across all expressions of your Oversoul.

Appendix C: Soulstream Lexicon

A living glossary of terms used throughout The Soul of Remembering Companion. These are not fixed definitions, but fluid keys—each may open differently for you depending on your own journey of remembering.

Alignment – The state of resonance between your human self, soul, and Oversoul. In alignment, action feels clear, flow is natural, and synchronicities increase.

Anchoring – The act of embodying a frequency so fully that it becomes stabilized in the physical realm. Often used to bring higher vibrational states into everyday life.

Ascension – The ongoing process of expanding consciousness and integrating higher frequencies into one's being. Not an escape from the physical, but an elevation within it.

Concurrent Expressions – Other lives of your Oversoul unfolding in different timelines, realms, or dimensions, experienced alongside your current incarnation.

Coherence – A state where thought, feeling, and action are harmonized, creating a powerful field for manifestation and healing.

Gaia – The sentient, living consciousness of Earth, holding her own evolutionary path alongside humanity's.

Integration – The process of weaving new insights, energies, or retrieved fragments into the whole of your being so they are lived, not just known.

Oversoul – The greater, multidimensional aspect of your being from which all incarnations emerge. It holds the full memory, wisdom, and purpose of your soulstream.

Parallel Timeline – An alternate unfolding of events where different choices or soul agreements are explored. Sometimes sensed in dreams or déjà vu experiences.

Remembering – The soul's act of returning to the awareness of its eternal truth. A process of calling home scattered fragments, awakening dormant codes, and restoring the full resonance of the Oversoul within the present incarnation. Remembering is not about learning something new, but recognizing and embodying what has always been known. It unfolds as a spiral, each return bringing deeper integration, and is lived through alignment of thought, heart, and action.

Soul Codes – Unique energetic imprints carried within your soul, containing memory, gifts, and purpose.

Soulstream – The continuum of your soul's existence across all incarnations, timelines, and realms—a river of consciousness flowing through eternity.

Walk-In – A soul exchange in which one soul departs a physical body and another enters, by mutual agreement, without physical death.

Whisper – A subtle nudge, image, or phrase from your Oversoul or guides, often recognized by its calm clarity and resonance in the heart.

Keywords such as these will deepen in meaning as you encounter them in the context of your own remembering. Return to this lexicon whenever you feel a term shifting for you—it is meant to grow with you.

Appendix D: Soundscapes of Remembrance

"Certain sounds are keys—when you hear them, doors within you open."

Sound is one of the most direct pathways to soul memory. Whether through frequency tones, ancient instruments, or natural soundscapes, these vibrations bypass the thinking mind and speak directly to the deeper self.

Below is a curated selection of sound frequencies and styles to support your journey of remembering. Each is paired with its purpose and suggested use.

- **432 Hz** – Known as the 'Heartbeat of the Earth,' this tuning aligns with natural frequencies found in nature. It promotes relaxation, emotional release, and a sense of homecoming.

- **528 Hz** – Often called the 'Love Frequency' or 'Miracle Tone.' Used for DNA repair, heart opening, and harmonizing the emotional body.

- **639 Hz** – Supports healthy relationships, compassion, and emotional communication. Ideal for mending bonds or cultivating new soul connections.

- **741 Hz** – Associated with clarity, detoxification, and releasing emotional blockages. A cleansing tone for both body and mind.

- **852 Hz** – Enhances spiritual insight and intuition. Assists in awakening higher consciousness and dissolving illusions.

- **Crystal Singing Bowls** – Each bowl resonates with a specific chakra, supporting alignment and deep energetic clearing.

- **Native Drumming** – A steady beat that entrains the brain into theta states, supporting journeying, grounding, and connecting with ancestral rhythms.

- **Ocean Waves** – Encourages emotional soothing and a return to the womb-like safety of Gaia's embrace.

- **Rainfall** – Calms the nervous system and helps to clear mental clutter, ideal for meditation or writing.

Reflection & Soul Notes

Prompted Reflections:
- Which tones or natural sounds feel most like 'home' to me?

- How does my body respond to each frequency?

- Do certain sounds evoke memories, images, or sensations from other lifetimes?

- What role could sound play in my daily spiritual practice?

Suggested Practice: Sound Immersion Meditation

1. Choose a soundscape or frequency from the list above.

2. Sit or lie down in a comfortable space where you won't be disturbed.

3. Close your eyes and breathe deeply, letting the sound wash through you.

4. Notice where it resonates in your body. Follow any images, emotions, or memories that arise.

5. After listening, journal your impressions.

Expanded Tip: Create a personal playlist of your most resonant tracks, arranged in an order that feels like a journey—beginning with grounding, moving through activation, and ending with integration.

The End

www.ingramcontent.com/pod-product-compliance
Lightning Source LLC
Chambersburg PA
CBHW070336240426

43665CB00045B/2120